La Négritude

La Négritude

An African Social Humanism

Dr Wacyf H Ghali

iUniverse

LA NÉGRITUDE
AN AFRICAN SOCIAL HUMANISM

iUniverse books may be ordered through booksellers or by contacting:

iUniverse
1663 Liberty Drive
Bloomington, IN 47403
www.iuniverse.com
844-349-9409

ISBN: 978-1-6632-6425-1 (sc)
ISBN: 978-1-6632-6426-8 (e)

Library of Congress Control Number: 2024912704

Print information available on the last page.

iUniverse rev. date: 07/30/2024

The design of the medallion, as shown on the FRONT COVER, was created by Josiah Wedgwood in 1787 as an important part of the anti-slavery campaign of the time. He was a prominent abolitionist and an English potter. He founded the Wedgwood Company, which is well-known to this day.

The Wedgwood medallion was the most famous image of a black person in all of 18th century art, which brought public attention to the quest of abolishing slavery.

Contents

Dedication

This book is dedicated to my ancestry. The longer I have lived, the more I know how much my ancestry has meant to me. My ancestry has taught me what Sir Nicholas Winton (1909-2015) once said so eloquently: "*that anything that is not actually impossible can be done, if one really sets one's mind to do it, and is determined that it shall be done*".

My roots are my ancestry, my faith, my values, my family, who I am today – all these attributes bundled into one package. In this respect, my ancestry and my faith have always pointed me to the fact that God has always been with me during good times as well as tough times, always reminding me of the verse in the Book of Isaiah which states "*For I am the Lord, your God, who takes hold of your right hand and says to you, Do not fear; for I will help you.*" (Isaiah 41:13)

In regard to my ancestry, I am reminded that, apart from my parents, one in particular was fundamental in ensuring that I understand that faith alone is the foundation of who I am as he, back then, created and embraced the family motto of "*Al-Motawakkal ilal Mota'ali*" which, in Latin, corresponds to "*In Deo Confido*" and in English means "*Trust In God*". This ancestor is Moallem Guirguis Ghali (born in Tahta, Egypt in 1775 and died in Zifta, Mansoura Province, Egypt in 1822).

As a way of recognizing and acknowledging him, a brief description of the man follows.

Guirguis Ghali was officially known as Moallem Ghali. Moallem was a title granted to someone deemed to have contributed significantly to Egyptian national life and (during Ghali's era) was the highest title given to a non-Muslim in Egypt. Moallem is an Arabic word meaning Master or Teacher (not unlike the Hebrew word rabbi but without any religious connotation).

Guirguis Ghali or Moallem Ghali is my direct ancestor (roughly 9th generation preceding me). He was the Prime Intendant of the Viceroy and ruler of Egypt, Mohammed Ali Pacha, in the early 1800s, and therefore, responsible for the entire civil administration of Egypt. Today, the title of Prime Intendant would almost be equivalent to Prime Minister (I say almost because the administrative responsibilities would, for instance, not include the Defense and Foreign Affairs portfolios).

In addition, on the 1st of May 1807 Pope Pie VII accorded Moallem Ghali "*Le Privilege de L'Oratoire Prive*", and on the 21st of August 1807 the same Pope granted him "ex-Audientia" the title of "*Chevalier de L'Eperon D'Or et Comte Palatin*". He was also the Chief of Copts from 1817 until his death in 1822 (Chief meaning as the chief of a tribe or ethnic group).

His death was a direct result of his assassination carried out by order of Ibrahim Pacha, one of the sons of the ruler of Egypt, who saw in Moallem Ghali a threat to his relationship with his father as well as because of the power he held as a non-member of the ruling family. The fact of his assassination is recorded in history books. However, the reason Ibrahim Pasha carried out the assassination is the subject of "*oral communication*" passed on within the family from one generation to another, from one person to another person.

Oral communication is an important tradition, especially in the Middle East and Africa, enabling matters of personal and/or historical significance to be transmitted by word-of-mouth. This method of communication is known as "*oral tradition*" or "*oral historical preservation*" because it preserves historical information based on meaningful personal experiences and opinions. A strong example is Alex Haley's 1977 Pulitzer Prize-winning book entitled "*Roots: The Saga of an American Family*", created as a result of oral tradition (historical preservation) followed by information obtained through research leading to further historical family facts.

On his tomb Moallem Ghali's epitaph, translated from Arabic, reads: "*Here lies the one who was regarded in glory and in splendor in the State of Egypt, like the ancient Joseph. His Spirit has returned to God and his body rests in this lonely mausoleum. The author of this epitaph stated to this tomb "Keep him with jealous care because he is precious*" (the word precious is the English descriptive meaning of the Arabic Coptic name Ghali). The epitaph was engraved on the tomb in 1824 and composed by Basilios Bey Ghali (1796-1847), the eldest son of Moallem Ghali – Basilios was the first Christian and the first Copt to receive the title of Bey (an Egyptian title of peerage), and was eventually appointed to the position that his father had prior to his assassination.

MOALLEM GHALI

Wacyf Ghali, June 10, 2024

Footnote:

"*Les Familles Coptes Du Caire: Famille Ghali*", by H.L. Rabino and published by Imprimerie D. Spada, 1937

"*Merveilles Biographique et Historiques*" du cheikh Abd el-Rahman al-Djabarti. Traduction Franciase, Le Caire, T. VII, 1892, pp. 273, 393, 397; T. VIII, 1895 pp. 170, 240, 275, 284; T. IX, 1896, pp. 78, 165, 167.

"*Histoire de l'Eglise d'Alexandrie*", by R.P. Georges Macaire, Le Caire, 1894, pp. 360-372 and 377-378.

"*Histoire de l'Egypte Sous Mohammed Aly*", by Felix Mengin, Paris, 1923, T. II, pp. 60-61 and 63; *op. cit* T. II, p. 247

"*Histoire de Mehmet Ali, Vice-Roi d'Egypte*", by Paul Mouriez, Paris, 1858, p. 32.

Extrait d'une letter du Consul de France Drovetti, au Ministere des Affaires Etrangeres a Paris, date d'Alexandrie, le 22 Mai 1822.

Indult (a privilege granted by the Pope) *du 1er Mai 1807*: Ex-Audientia Smi Nri Pii Divina Providentia PP: VII:habita per me infrum Sacrae Congnis De Propaganda Fide Praefectum Die Prima Maji 1807.

Lettre du Pope Pie VII a Moallem Ghali et Philotheos Yakoub (cousin-germain de Moallem Ghali), 15 Juillet 1807. Extract from the Archives of the Propaganda at Rome (Udienze di N.S. Vol. 45. Fol.365 v.).

"*Le Statut Personnel des Non Musulmans*", Le Caire, 1937; "*La Protection Religieuse En Egypte*", Le Caire, 1937. Les deux livres sont écrits par Ragheb Bey Ghali

"*The Story of the Church of Egypt: Being an Outline of the History of the Egyptians Under Their Successive Masters From The Roman Conquest Until Now*" by Edith Louisa Butcher, published in1897 by Smith, Elder, & Co., England, pp ii 360, 366, 367.

"*Copts And Moslems Under British Control; A Collection Of Facts And A Résumé Of Authoritative Opinions On The Coptic Question*" by Mikhail, Kyriakos, published in 1911 by Smith, Elder & Co., London, England, pp XV, 146

Epigraph

An epigraph is defined as "a brief quotation or saying at the beginning of a *presentation, book, or chapter, intended to suggest its theme*"

Creation of Nations: The creation of languages, referred to as language diversity, at The Tower of Babel, was the driving force in the eventual formation of ethnic groups and then nations. That happened when **(1)** the Big Bang of Language Diversity occurred which formally caused the establishment of groups, each with a common and different speech; and **(2)** every group with a common speech eventually dispersed and migrated to different geographical areas to fill the earth. Thus, marking the origin of ethnic groups and the eventual creation of nations on earth (Genesis Chapter 11:1- 9).

Learning from History: The following quote, by an **Unknown Person,** is worth posting here as it is a reminder for everyone that, no matter what, there is a lot to learn from history, humanity's past. Here is the quote: *History is not there for you to like or dislike. It is there for you to learn from it. And if it offends you even better. Because then, you are less likely to repeat it. It is not yours to erase or destroy. It belongs to all of us."*

Karl Marx (1818-1883): Karl Marx is considered to be the father of Communism. He, and Friedrich Engels, wrote The Communist Manifesto which was published in February 1848. A key principle in the Manifesto states that "*the first battlefield is the rewriting of history … take away the heritage of a people and they are easily persuaded.*"

This quoted statement is considered, by many experts, to be one of the first principles of evil. It has been used (along with others) to help implement a revolutionary class struggle against faith in general but specifically Judeo-Christian values, as well as capitalism, the institution of marriage, and democratic principles, in order to install a communist based society. See article in *Renew America* by Ellis Washington issued on May 2, 2015, and entitled "*On Karl Marx and the First Principle of Evil.*"

The Policy of Grabbing (reflects the essence of colonialism & colonial wars): From the 1952 movie entitled "The Big Sky", minutes 36:08 on Amazon Prime. In the movie Zeb Callaway recounts the tale of the first white men who explored the Missouri River in the 19th century. Zeb said "*Her people, the proud Blackfoot Indians, ain't gonna let no white men spoil their country. The only fear is the white man's sickness called GRABS. White men don't see nothing pretty unless they want to grab it. The more they grab, the more they want to grab. It's like a fever and they can't get cured. The only thing for them to do is to keep on grabbing till everything belongs to white men and then they start grabbing from each other. Reckon Blackfoot Indians got no reason to love nothing white?*"

George Orwell (1903-1950)
"*In time of deceit to tell the truth is a revolutionary act.*"

Wisdom from Abraham Lincoln (1809-1865)
"*When effecting change, call on the past. Relate to the present, and then use them both to provide a link to the future.*"

Acknowledgement and Image Credit

The inscription "*Am I not a Man and a Brother*?", on the medallion created by Josiah Wedgwood in 1787 (as shown on the Cover Page) became the catchphrase of British and American abolitionists. Medallions were even sent to Benjamin Franklin, one of the Founding Fathers of the U.S.A., in 1788, who was then president of the Pennsylvania Abolition Society.

Although the kneeling black figure looks docile and unpretentious in prayer, the image nonetheless helped to inspire and rally support for the abolitionist cause. Benjamin Franklin had declared that the medallion's effectiveness was "*equal to that of the best written Pamphlet, in procuring favor to the oppressed People.*"

Who were the Abolitionists? The Encyclopedia Britannica (2024 edition) summarizes the answer as follows: "*They were an organized movement, which started in the 1780s, in Western Europe and the United States of America. Their sole purpose was to end the practice of slavery in Britain and in America, as well as the Atlantic slave trade that supported it. The first organized group that was formed to end enslavement in America began in Philadelphia in 1775.*"

In addition, it is important to be thankful for the likes of William Wilberforce (1759-1833, who was a British politician, philanthropist, and a leader of the movement to abolish the slave trade), John Newton (1725-1807, who wrote the famous hymn "*Amazing Grace*" based on his experience related to the slave trade, and who helped Wilberforce in his quest to abolish it), USA President Abraham Lincoln (1809-1865, who fought a Civil War to preserve the Union and to abolish slavery in America and won), and many others who dedicated their lives to ensure that people (human beings) were freed from bondage and had the same equal rights as any individual anywhere in the world.

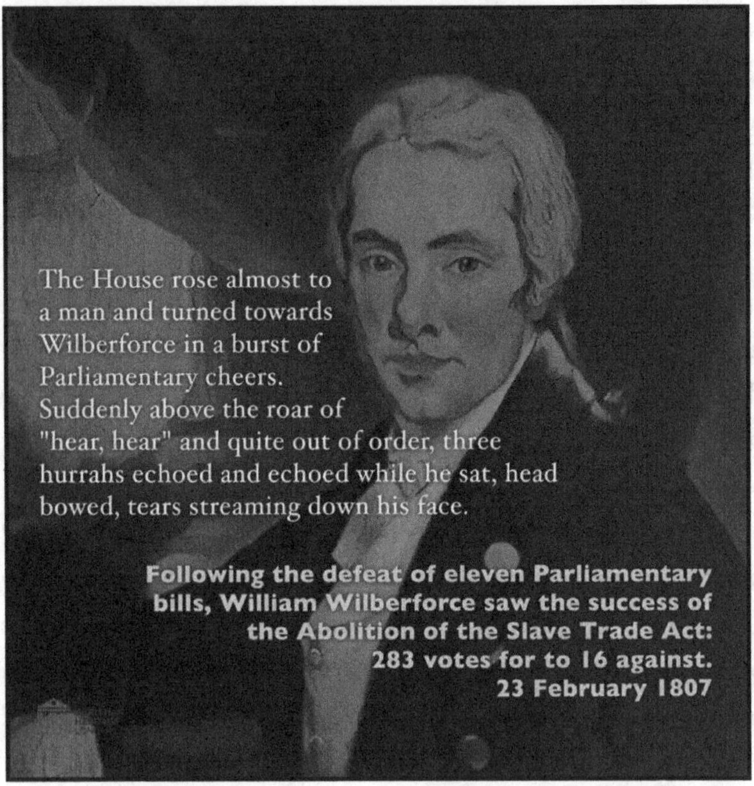
The House rose almost to
a man and turned towards
Wilberforce in a burst of
Parliamentary cheers.
Suddenly above the roar of
"hear, hear" and quite out of order, three
hurrahs echoed and echoed while he sat, head
bowed, tears streaming down his face.
Following the defeat of eleven Parliamentary
bills, William Wilberforce saw the success of
the Abolition of the Slave Trade Act:
283 votes for to 16 against.
23 February 1807

Following the defeat of eleven Parliamentary bills, William Wilberforce saw the success of the "Abolition of the Slave Trade Act" on 23 February 1807.

William Wilberforce (1759-1833) finally ended slavery throughout the British Empire in 1833. The Adam Smith Institute.

Three special persons whom I also owe a debt of gratitude for having influenced me to pen this book because of their writings, their courage and determination, their coining of the words "La Négritude", and the movement that developed bearing these words, are Leopold Senghor (1906-2001, an African poet, politician, and cultural theorist who, for two decades 1960 to 1980, served as the first President of Senegal after its independence from France, and who was the major theoretician of Negritude); Aimé Césaire (1913-2008, who was a Francophone and French poet, an Afro-Caribbean author and politician from the region of Martinique); and, Léon-Gontran Damas (1912-1978, born in French Guiana, who was a French poet, writer, and politician, and a founder of the Négritude Movement).

Moreover, I take this opportunity to thank iUniverse Publishing, Inc. for being involved in publishing my book, and the iUniverse Team (consisting of the Check-In Coordinator & Concierge, the Editorial Dept, the Design Dept, the Compliance Dept, etc.) assigned to me to guide, counsel, and help me through the process of reaching my aspirations as a writer. This Team has acted, one might say, as a gatekeeper between author and audience.

In regard to the images or photos contained in this book, which were obtained from Getty Images under iUniverse agreement, and the Public Domain via the likes of Google, Microsoft Bing, and others, I take this opportunity to thank all those who have created and published such important and meaningful works, and for allowing people like me to be able to use them.

Finally, it is not possible to write a book such as this one without researching extensively, and eventually drawing or adopting ideas from the works of others. Therefore, I would like to express my appreciation to the many scholars and experts (e.g., teachers, historians, writers) whose work has helped me in the production of this book, as shown in my many and diverse footnotes and the bibliography. It is obvious that, over the years, I have been able to collect important and meaningful material to write this book. In the process, I have attempted to give credit to others where needed and required. However, if I have forgotten to name a source of information for my book I apologize in advance.

Wacyf Ghali
June 10, 2024

Preface

Originally written on December 3, 1963, as a Term Paper for the American University in Cairo, Egypt, it was then revised into a shorter version, translated in French, and published in the Egyptian Francophone magazine "*Image*" in two issues with the first entitled "*Le Development de la Négritude*" (October 18-24, 1969) and the second entitled "*L'Ideologie de la Négritude et son Application*" (November 15-21, 1969).

Though I am not a Social Humanist but rather (if I must be labeled) a Judeo-Christian Humanist, I have been attracted to the theme and ideology of "La Négritude" as it applies to the African context, since my years at university in Egypt and later in the U.S.A. Notwithstanding this, it is especially as a result of encouragement by close friends with whom I had shared my initial work, and who thought I should publish it, that the original work was revised, further updated, and expanded as a book into its current written form.

The subject of my writing is entitled "*La Négritude: An African Social Humanism*". La Négritude are obviously French words, and were originally coined in the 1930's as a valid strategy for "*la resistance*" against French colonialists. In English, Négritude means "Blackness", "Negroid".

The word Négritude is an invented idea formed from the French word "nègre" (meaning black or negro in French). Its use was a method, a way, of empowering a social ethnic group. Therefore, La Négritude was used in reference to being proud to be black, proud of being a Negro (the true and correct word for defining an African black man's or woman's ethnicity). Instead of being disrespectful, the word Négritude became meaningful and beautiful in terms of what it portrayed and still portrays, what it represents (and how it helped start a movement to free Black Africa from colonialism – specifically French Colonialism).

We know that with the impact of slavery and colonialism, the traditional Negro-African society was transformed into a modern society so different from the old one that many expressed a loss of identity: culturally, politically, and economically. In addition, artificial boundaries were created by the colonialists which totally disregarded ethnic, tribal, and parochial units creating modern states that, in many instances, caused ethnic tensions, which went as far as causing civil wars with the purpose of tribal ethnic cleansing. It is a fact that there are very few ethnic groups (or races, as some would prefer to call them) that have experienced the same extent of slavery, racialism, and colonialization.

La Négritude is founded on a Social Humanism which attempts to redefine and re-identify the Negro-African society and values existing before, and during, the era of colonialism. It was meant to instill a sense of security and unity among the people, with the understanding that adopting positive changes from outside Negro-Africa and incorporating them into the Negro-African persona could allow for positive growth and development without fear of destroying that African character, that African personality.

On the subject of La Négritude, there is lots to write about – a lot more than what is in this Book. Nevertheless, I have preferred to try to be concise, specific, and simple in reflecting the issues. I leave it to others to add and/or complete the story, if need be, from the perspective of my writing.

Wacyf Ghali – June 10, 2024

Chapter I

Introduction to Africa and La Négritude

A. Setting The Stage

Africa is the world's second largest and second most populous continent after Asia at about 30.2 million square kilometers or 11.7 million square miles including adjacent islands (e.g., Madagascar, Zanzibar, Mauritius, Seychelles). It covers 6 percent of the earth's total surface area and 20.4 percent of its total land area.(1) With 1.3 billion people in 2019, it accounts for about 16% of the world's human population.(2)

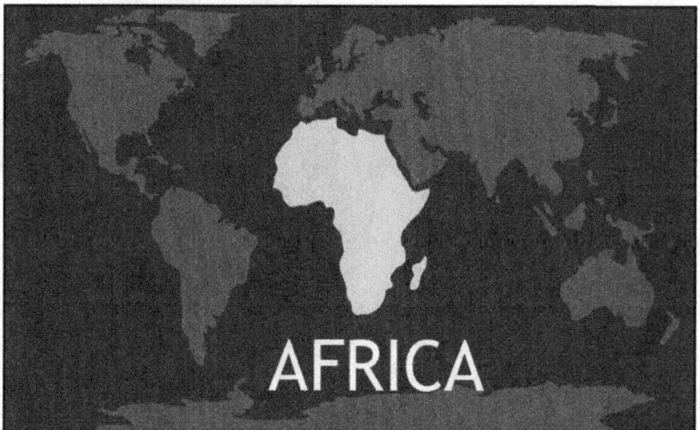

The continent is surrounded by the Mediterranean Sea to the North, both the Suez Canal and the Red Sea along the Sinai

Peninsula to the northeast, the Indian Ocean to the southeast, and the Atlantic Ocean to the West.

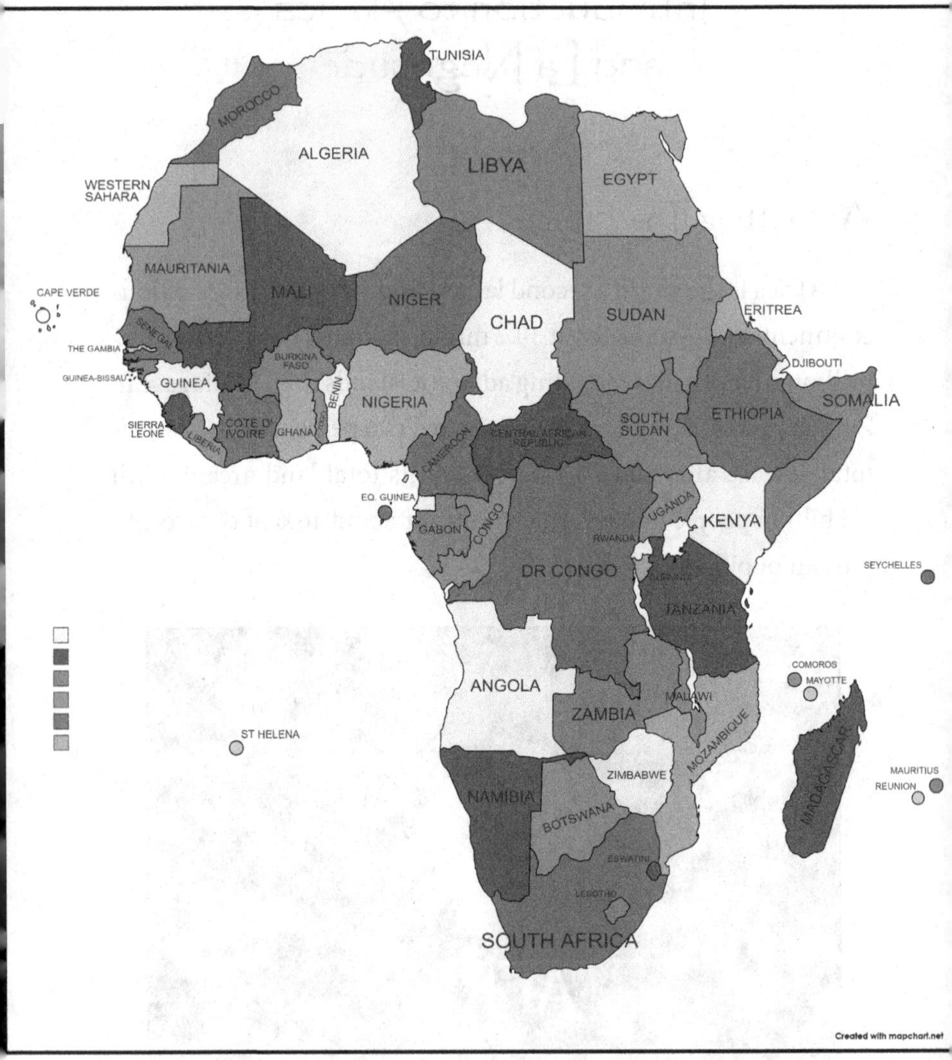

Countries of Africa (including the island nations)

Africa hosts 54 sovereign countries, and is twice the size of the South American continent.[3] Its population is the youngest among all the continents with the median age in 2012 at 19.7, when the worldwide median age was 30.4.[(4)(5)] In addition, it has a large diversity of ethnicities (mainly tribes), cultures, and languages.

Africa's diverse tribal and ethno-linguistic groupings are in the thousands of tribes - about 3,000 of them speaking more than 2,000 different languages and dialects. For example, Nigeria with an estimated population of over 206 million has more than 500 tribes; and Zambia with a population of about 17 million has 72 different tribes.[(6)]

B. The Plight Of Africa

Although it has abundant natural resources, Africa remains the world's poorest and most underdeveloped of the continents. In today's era, it is the result of a variety of causes that may include corrupt governments that have often committed serious human rights violations, failed central planning, high levels of illiteracy, lack of access to foreign capital, and frequent tribal and military conflicts (ranging from guerilla warfare to genocide).[(7)]

Thus, from a general point of view, it is not surprising that Africa today can be identified as a land of wealth as well as a land of poverty.

African nations-states typically fall toward the bottom of any list measuring economic activity, such as HDI (Human Development Index), income per capita or per capita GDP (Gross Domestic Product), despite a wealth of natural resources.

Poverty in Africa means the lack of provision to satisfy the basic human needs. One of the key factors contributing to poverty in Africa is economic instability. High rates of unemployment, income inequality, and economic policies that sometimes fail to prioritize the needs of the most vulnerable citizen. Another issue is that, in many African countries, like many places in the world, a small percentage of the population controls a significant portion of the nation's wealth. This leaves the majority of people struggling to meet their needs.

According to the United Nations' Human Development Report Index 2023-24, issued in early 2024, the bottom 30 ranked nations (163rd to 193rd) were all African.[(8)]

Poverty, illiteracy, malnutrition, and inadequate water supply and sanitation, as well as poor health, affect a considerable proportion of the people who reside in the African continent.[(9)] In its October 17, 2018, Press Release, The World Bank (Washington D.C., USA) announced revised global poverty estimates based on a new international poverty line of US$2.15 per day (versus the previous measure of US$1.90).[(10a)]

Economic advances around the world mean that while fewer people live in extreme poverty still about 42 percent of the world's population (or 3.4 billion people) struggles to meet basic needs. In regard to Sub-Sahara Africa, a third of the countries in the region experienced negative income growth for the bottom 40 percent of their populations. The region with the largest number of extreme poor, Africa saw its population nearly double between 1990 and 2015, with one of the largest increases in population being for those living on less than $3.20 and more than $1.90. The poor suffered from multiple deprivations such as low consumption levels and lack of access to education and basic infrastructure services.[(10b)]

The continent is believed to hold 90% of the world's cobalt,

90% of its platinum, 50% of its gold, 98% of its chromium, 70% of its tantalite, 64% of its manganese, one-third of its uranium, 13% of the global copper production, 12% of the world's oil, and 8% of its natural gas reserves. In a nutshell, according to the United Nations, Africa is home to about 30% of the world's non-renewable natural resources.[11]

Further statistics point to the fact that The Democratic Republic of the Congo (DRC) has 70% of the world's coltan, a mineral used in the production of tantalum capacitors for electronic devices such as cell phones. The DRC also has more than 30% of the world's diamond reserves. Guinea is the world's largest exporter of bauxite.[12] As the growth in Africa has been driven by primarily services and not manufacturing or agriculture, it has seen economic growth but without important job creation and without improving the education in poverty level areas.[13]

A Harvard University study led by professor Dr. Calestous Juma (1953-2017, a well-known Kenyan scientist and academic, specializing in sustainable development) showed that Africa could feed itself by making the transition from importer to self-sufficiency. "*African agriculture is at the crossroads,*" says Dr. Juma. Juma also states, "*We have come to the end of a century of policies that favored Africa's export of raw materials and importation of food. Africa is starting to focus on agricultural innovation as its new engine for regional trade and prosperity.*"[14]

Africa today is a sad continent. The only way that this continent and its people can be helped is by facing up to the truth and stop living in a make-believe world that all will be well if only money is poured into Africa.[15]

As mentioned earlier, Africa in general can be identified as a land of wealth and a land of poverty. So... what would unlock Africa's potential and allow its people to create wealth for themselves? How would it develop economically? What is the missing ingredient that could transform Africa into a prosperous continent? Does it need to re-establish traditional African values? Should it adopt foreign values (non-African) that worked well elsewhere? Or should it combine African traditional values with compatible foreign ones that would help re-energize the African persona and allow it to be motivated and challenged to break the deadlock that it currently faces?

C. What Is It That Could Unlock Africa's Great Potential?

Economic development depends upon good governance. From a general point of view, this is the ingredient which has been missing for far too long. It is the change that could unlock Africa's potential - depending on how that change is defined, put into an effective plan, and then implemented with determination in a constructive and disciplined manner. And, that is a responsibility that can only be met by Africans for Africans.[16]

In order to achieve the required economic development, African nation-states would need to embrace an ideology which would form the basis of economic, social, and political policy that would translate into a program, a plan, to be implemented with good governance, and consequently improve the future. It would offer to either make changes in society based on new principles and values, or keep to a set of ideals where conformity already exists such as in the tribal system, or stand by a mix of both.

The best advice to move forward was given by Lord Norman Tebbit, a British Peer, a former chairman of the British Conservative party, and a member of former British Prime Minister Mrs. Margaret Thatcher's cabinet. When on a visit to South Africa in 1994, he said: "... *we have forgotten the order in which things have to be done. The first priority is the essence – the economy. The second priority is law and order, the freedom from the threat of violence. The third priority is freedom, the ability to order one's own affairs. The fourth priority, the last on the list, is democracy... but too many people think that the list works in reverse. It doesn't.*"[17]

Absolutely correct, only when the economy gets going, and law and order is effectively in place to protect the people from violence and other offenses can freedoms and eventually democracy flourish.

D. The Possible Answer

So ... what is the possible answer?

Africans must seek to adjust their political and economic systems to African conditions and their distinctive African style of life. They also must focus on the ethical-humanistic principles and values that existed in pre-colonial times which would allow an emphasis on the satisfaction of simple human needs and the welfare of the community (which is much needed) rather than, for example, the rapid industrialization of the society.

Therefore, a new and well-defined framework (a plan of action) needs to be established based on the socio-economic-historical conditions, past and present, so that political and economic problems are solved, so that there is a positive and encouraging future – and that will tend to involve tremendously intense determination and undertaking in order to achieve the required results.

With the advent of colonialism, the traditional Negro-African society was transformed into a modern society, so different from the old one that many expressed a loss of identity. With independence, therefore, came a need to reconstruct the Negro-African nation, whose artificial boundaries were created by the colonialists and disregarded ethical, ethnic, and parochial units.

In addition, there was a need to identify oneself with the Negro-African society that prevailed before or during the era of colonialism. In other words, it eventually resulted in a revival that entailed a selection of the past: a selection made not only in terms of the requirements of the present but of the plans for the future. Hence, it was a reassertion of the values of the Negro-African society, the creation of an African unity which could instill a sense of security that could allow Sub-Sahara Africa to adopt changes from outside the continent (as for example technological change) without fear that these adoptions would destroy the African character – the African personality.

One of the ways to fulfill the task of safeguarding the Negro-African values and the personality of the Black man is through the Ideology of La Négritude.

The spokespersons of La Négritude believe that through it Negro-Africans would be able to secure an independence from the European elements of dominance; and, attempt to regain the African identity, unify the diverse ethnicities, and improve the Negro-African's abilities through his or her own effort.

Therefore, La Négritude through establishing a modernized system of governance, evolving from the tribal system with a Chief and a Council of Elders, would in effect meet the order of priorities Lord Norman Tebbit established and stressed (mentioned above). In doing so, a step-by-step approach to governing effectively could pave the way for democratic institutions to flourish in the future.

- - -

To understand the African character (its persona) and how La Négritude developed, this book will be explaining - in the chapters to come - many historic, social, economic, and political aspects that will point to the reasons why and how such an ideology came to be.

Footnote:

1. *Sayre, April Pulley (1999),* Africa, *Twenty-First Century Books.*
2. "*Population of Africa (2019)*" by Worldometers – a provider of global statistics.
3. "*2020 Alphabetical List of All African Countries*" By Angela Thompsell (Professor of British and African History), published by Thought Co. – an Internet company.
4. "*Five Ways The World Will Look Dramatically Different in 2100*", The Washington Post August 17, 2015
5. *Abdoulie Janneh (April 2012). "Item 4 of the provisional agenda – General debate on national experience in population matters: adolescents and youth (Pdf). United Nations Economic Commission For Africa. Retrieved 15 December 2015.*
6. Sidney & Shirley Robbins, Africa: A Continent in Agony – We Accuse, (Revised 2012 as an eBook, Capsal Publishers), location pages 215, 235.
7. Richard Sandbrook, *The Politics of Africa's Economic Stagnation*, Cambridge University Press, 1985
8. "*United Nations Development Program*", Website: http://hdr.undp.org/

9. "World Bank Updates Poverty Estimates for Developing World". *World Bank. 26 August 2008. Archived from the original on 19 May 2010.*

10a&10b. *"Nearly Half of the World Lives on Less Than $5.50 A Day."* The World Bank, Washington D.C., USA. Press Release No. 2019/044/DEC-GPV. October 17, 2018. The World Bank, Washington D.C., USA

11. *"All Africa: Developed Countries' Leverage on the Continent"*. AllAfrica.com. February 7, 2008.

12. *"China tightens grip on Africa with $4.4bn lifeline for Guinea junta"*. The Times. October 13, 2009.

13. *"The African Decade?."* Ilmas Futehally. Strategic Foresight Group, and Economic Report in Africa 2004 (Substantive session 28 June-23 July 2004), United Nations. And, Human Development Report 2023-24. *"Breaking the gridlock: Reimaging cooperation in a polarized world."* United Nations Development Program, 13 March 2024.

14. *"Africa Can Feed Itself in a Generation, Experts Say"*, Science Daily, December 3, 2010.

15. "Africa: A Continent in Agony – We Accuse", by Sidney & Shirley Robbins, Capsual Publishers, Published 2012, eBook Location page 118.

16. "Ibid", by Sidney & Shirley Robbins, eBook Location page 787.

17. "Ibid", page 118.

Chapter II

All Came from One Family - Origin of Nations & of Mankind

A. The Truth, Why With A Capital "T"

In today's world, it would seem that Mankind (or, as some would prefer to say, The Human Race or Humankind) has declared that Truth is not that important anymore. Nevertheless, human beings still value truth. They agree that it is better to tell the truth than to lie. But ... truth today tends to be declared from a small "t" point of view and not Truth with a capital "T" – simply put, the capital "T" in Truth has declined in importance at about the same time that people began turning their backs on God, with many declaring He does not exist.[1]

It is obvious that we live in a world that tends to believe that "*what is true for you may not be true for me*" or that "*truth is whatever makes me or you happy*" or that "*what you or I believe doesn't matter, as long as we are sincere*". Like so many other erroneous accounts, expressions, or attitudes, these types of statements mislead us as they take us away from the truth, and as they end up promoting deception – that is, deception (or falsehood) that finds its way in our everyday life. In other words, stated differently, many today do not believe in absolute truth, truth with a capital "T"; and many others (whether knowingly or not) tend to be falsifiers of information.

This is in spite of the fact that God resolved to send His

message to the world He created, a message filled with everything He wanted people to know: about Himself, about creation and salvation, about themselves and their future. Can you envision God choosing forty different authors from all walks of life (fishermen, shepherds, a doctor, and a tax collector), from three different continents (Africa, Asia, and Europe), writing in three different languages (Hebrew, Aramaic, and Greek), over a period of 1,500 years **MERELY** to convey a message of abstractions and generalities from which people could read and come up with their own so-called truths? What good would that be, or in fact do?

So, in regard to the Truth, God's Truth, where did we all come from? Who settled the continent of Africa? And, where did the name Africa and the word Negro originate or come from?

Let us find out from this chapter, at the least, some details that could be thought provoking, inciteful, and meaningful in regard to finding answers to those questions. Furthermore, this chapter, as well as the next one, will also establish the foundation from which the name of "Blackness" or "La Negritude" develops into a colonial and post-colonial movement that addresses the concerns of the African people and, at the same time, demonstrates to the world that Blackness is not a prejudiced word, but indeed a word that beautifully reflects pride in one's ethnicity.

In this context, **this** chapter will address the following points:

- What Is the Table of Nations, and Why Is It Important?
- The Lineage of Ham, Ancestor of the Negro and Other Ethnic Groups
- Cush Son of Ham: The Man and The Land

while the next chapter (Chapter III) will explain the "origin of the name Africa and the word Negro", and is specifically entitled:

- The Name Africa: The Never Ending Debate
- The Word Negro: Where Did It Come From?

B. The Table of Nations: With Emphasis on Ham, Ancestor of the Negro Ethnic Group

1. What Is The Table of Nations?

The roots of the nations, **broadly referred to as The Table of Nations** or *Origines Gentium*[(2)] is a genealogy of the sons of Noah, according to the Hebrew Bible (Genesis 10:9), and their dispersion or migrations throughout the earth after the Biblical Flood.[(3)]

As Marcus Kalisch observed in his Historical and Critical Commentary of the Hebrew Bible (also referred to as the Old Testament),[(4)] "*The earliest historiography consists almost entirely of genealogies: they are most frequently the medium of explaining the connection and descent of tribes and nations, inserting where appropriate brief historical notes.*"

There is no question that when we see history as God sees it, in its totality and at the end of time, we discover that the Table of Nations is a fundamental and important clue to determining and interpreting its meaning (i.e., the meaning of history). In fact, it serves this purpose well because it has a structure which does not agree with what might be called ill-suited modern attempts to redefine the inter-relationships of the people of this world but, rather, is based on Truth.

For example, in contrast to contemporary attempts to redefine inter-personal relationships, we have the opinion of the famous Professor Emil F. Kautzsch who wrote: "*The so-called Table of Nations remains, according to all results of monumental explorations, an ethnographic original document of the first rank which nothing can replace.*"(5)

In short, Chapter 10 of The Book of Genesis, commonly known as **The Table of Nations,** is a unique document in the world as it is invaluable in deciphering the nations using genealogies mentioned throughout the Bible. Why? Here are key examples:

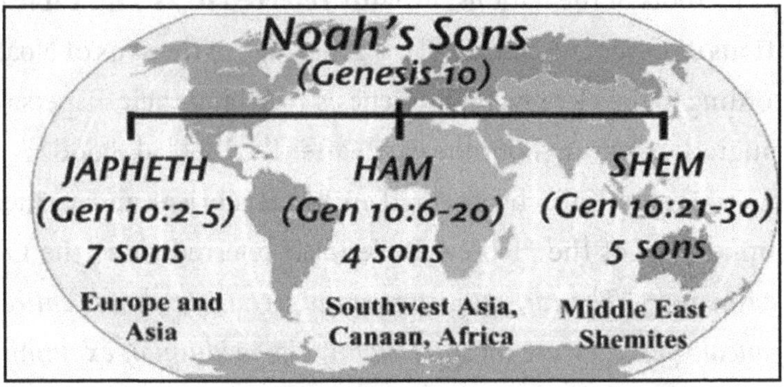

Japheth	*Ham*	*Shem*
Intellectual: Scientific And Philosophical	*Physical: Great Artisans and Builders*	*Spiritual: Great Religions*

- ➢ It starts by dividing the Human Race or Mankind into three families (Japheth, Ham, Shem) in a way which does not agree with, or is contrary to modern concepts of racial groupings; **BUT** that establishes and offers a much clearer insight into the framework of history as shown, for instance, in the chart and map below.

Many secular ethnologists today consider that race is commonly thought of as being only three divisions of Mankind: the Caucasian (loosely white ethnicity), Negroid (loosely black ethnicity) and Mongoloid (loosely yellow ethnicity). Traditionally, however, Biblical scholars have concluded that the three divisions of Mankind are the progeny of Noah's three sons: Japheth (the father of the Caucasians), Ham (the father of the Negroids), and Shem (the father of the Mongoloids).[(6)]

- The Table lists the patriarchal founders of 70 plus nations, as shown in the chart below, who descended from Noah through his three sons Shem, Ham and Japheth: **37%** descend from Shem, **43%** from Ham, and **20%** from Japheth. The 32nd verse of Genesis Chapter 10 sums up the chapter perfectly: "*These are the families of the sons of Noah, according to their genealogies, by their nations; and out of these the nations were separated on the earth after the flood.*" Genesis chapter 11 recounts their division at Babel.

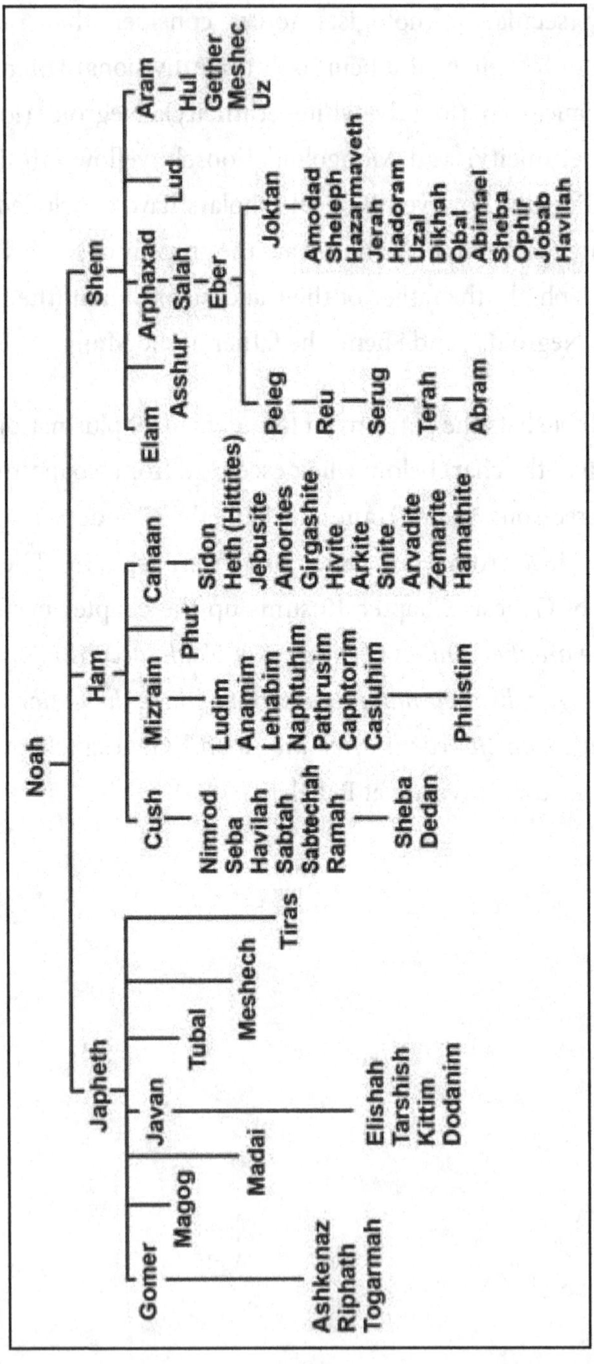

From Microsoft Bing: In Ancient Charts of "The Table of Nations".

Biblical history indicates that from Creation to the destruction of the Tower of Babel there was one language (approx. date 2275 BCE, based on the Hebrew Masoretic Text) which meant that all mankind spoke the same language until Babel. Obviously, this is completely contradictory to the theory of evolution which teaches that language evolved from animal sounds (such as grunts, groans, roars, clucks, etc.) to speech, and finally to language.

The act of confusing (or even refuting) the Biblical narrative regarding historical records of Mankind's languages, which indicated that many different languages were created and that each family of people had their own separate language, generated a significant divide between creationists and evolutionists. This divide was not based, for example, on skin color or physical characteristics, but on familial relationships – meaning a family or tribe of people with a given common language, separated from other groups speaking different languages.

As the people began to group themselves together, based on their common language, they began to migrate in all directions away from Babel. At Babel, they were a homogeneous people, but with God giving them different languages, they separated and in time became heterogeneous.

Because of their disobedience, God "confounded" their language and scattered them over all the earth (Genesis 11:7-8). The scattering of these groups all over the earth, which created genetic isolation, is the real cause for the origin of modern races of people.[7]

In other words, it is at Babel (which in today's term is located in the Land of Shinar about 80 km south of Baghdad, Iraq) that the "**Big Bang" of Language Diversity** occurred resulting in a multitude of languages being created from one. Consequently, the dispersion of people occurred to the different corners of the world, in separate groups with each group having their own distinctive language which was the catalyst that formed and established ethnic groups and eventually the nations.

- The list of 70 plus names introduces for the first time several well-known ethnonyms (a name applied to a given ethnic group) and toponyms (the study of proper names of places, their origins, and meanings) which are important to geographers and historians.

  For example, the 18th century German scholars at the "Gottingen School of History" derived the ethnic terminology of Semites, Hamites, and Japhetites, from Noah's three sons Shem, Ham, and Japheth. In addition, names of certain of Noah's grandsons were used to identify peoples and nations: the ancient nations called Elamites, Assyrians, Arameans, Cushites, and Canaanites were derived respectively from the names of Elam, Ashur, Aram, Cush, and Canaan. Likewise, from the sons of Canaan named Heth, Jebus, and Amorus were derived the Hittites, Jebusites, and Amorites. Further descendants of Noah include Eber from Shem (from whom the name "Hebrews" was coined); the hunter-king Nimrod of the Land of Shinar (Iraq today) from Cush; and the Philistines and Egyptians from Mizrayim(8)

- The majority of Bible scholars and Bible historians agree that[9]:

  - Descendants of **Shem** stayed in the Middle East. These include the Hebrews, Persians Assyrians, and Arabs.
  - Descendants of **Ham** include the Egyptians, Ethiopians, Canaanites, Phoenicians, and Hittites. His descendants appear to be the first to fill the earth, as they were the early settlers of Africa, Asia, Australia, the South Pacific, and the Americas.
  - Descendants of **Japheth** migrated into Europe and parts of Central Asia. For example, the Greeks, Romans, Spanish, Celts, Scythians, and Medes were Japheth's descendants.
  - Some **people groups merged** to form one nation, as did the Persians (Shem) and the Medes (Japheth), which later became the Medo-Persian Empire under king Cyrus (550 BCE).
  - Many nations or peoples were **named after an ancestor**. The Romans, and their capital city, were named after Romulus. Israelis and their country are named after their forefather Israel (Jacob). Briton originated from Brutus (a descendant of Elisha).

Attaching the name of a leader to his people and his empire appears often in Ancient Near Eastern history. The Table of Nations in Genesis 10 illustrates this principle, whereby every land was named after its first successful settler: Canaanites were named after Ham's son, Canaan; the Assyrians were named after Shem's son Asshur; the Egyptians were named Mizr in Arabic, after Mizraim, son of Ham; and so on.

In conclusion, this Table of Nations is a unique and priceless document. It makes a justifiable claim of completeness for the whole human race, and supplies us with insights into the relationships of the earliest people known to us, which would be quite lost if it was not for Genesis Chapters 10 and 11.

The expert opinion by well-known ethnologist Professor Kautzsch of Halle stated that "*The so-called Table of Nations remains, according to all results, of monumental explorations, an ethnographic original document of the first rank which nothing can replace.*"(10) How true.

We come, finally, to the question of the date of this document.

Traditionally the Table has been viewed as a self-contained early record, incorporated into the Book of Genesis, along with other early material such as the patriarchal accounts. It is understood that Genesis was assembled into its present form at the time of the Exodus (say around 1400 B.C.). The Table of Nations being a genuinely early record, incorporated with other early material into what we now call Genesis (the root word being origin, beginning, or birth), is a realistic and credible position. There is hardly any doubt that we have in this ethnographical section of Genesis one of the most valuable records of its kind.(10)

Obviously, it would not be appropriate to pretend that the information gathered here is in any sense complete. The subject is too vast and too deep for that. The intention, after all, is merely to present to the serious historical and geographical researcher a definite framework that can be built upon and added to as more information comes to light; and, in the process, vindicate a record that has assumed for far too long to be nothing more than what Bill Cooper would call "a pious fiction".(11)

2. The Lineage of Ham, Ancestor of the Negro and Other Ethnic Groups

Our focus in this section, and the next, of this chapter, is on Ham Son of Noah and on Cush son of Ham and grandson of Noah. Rather than write and describe the full particulars of all of the sons of Noah, it is now important to specifically turn to Ham and Cush, the ancestors of the Black People, with the required detail, in order to understand their roots and history ... and ultimately, the Negroid Ethnic Group of people that today prevail in most of Africa.

Ham is the youngest of Noah's three sons (Japheth being the oldest and then Shem the second oldest). Ham's sons number four, namely Cush (Ethiopia), Mizraim (Egypt), Put (Libya), and lastly, Canaan (Canaanites are believed to be the first settlers in what became known as Israel). Ham is a name of Hebrew origin, and can mean "burnt", "black", or "hot". It might be said he had a dark tan from the Sun or simply that he was dark-skinned. Cush means "black" in Hebrew and is sometimes used in referring to the ancient Ethiopians.(12)

It is through the lineage of Ham that most of Africa, parts of the Middle East, and Southwest Asia, and other parts of the world that his descendants are clearly noticeable. The Hamitic people (as Ham's descendants were known) were the first to reach the far and distant lands of the world, preparing the way for the future. Their inventions and discoveries made a significant impact on the world, and provided inspiration for those to follow. They were known to be great artisans and builders but also polytheists - contrary to Japheth whose descendants were intellectually scientific and philosophical but also polytheists, and Shem whose descendants were spiritual and therefore proponents of great religions.[13]

It is meaningful that ancient historians wrote about **The Land of Ham**. For example, Ham's descendants are interpreted by Flavius Josephus (a first-century Romano-Jewish historian and military leader) and Herodotus (484 – 425 BCE, an ancient Greek historian, considered "The Father of History") as having populated Africa and adjoining parts of Asia.[14]

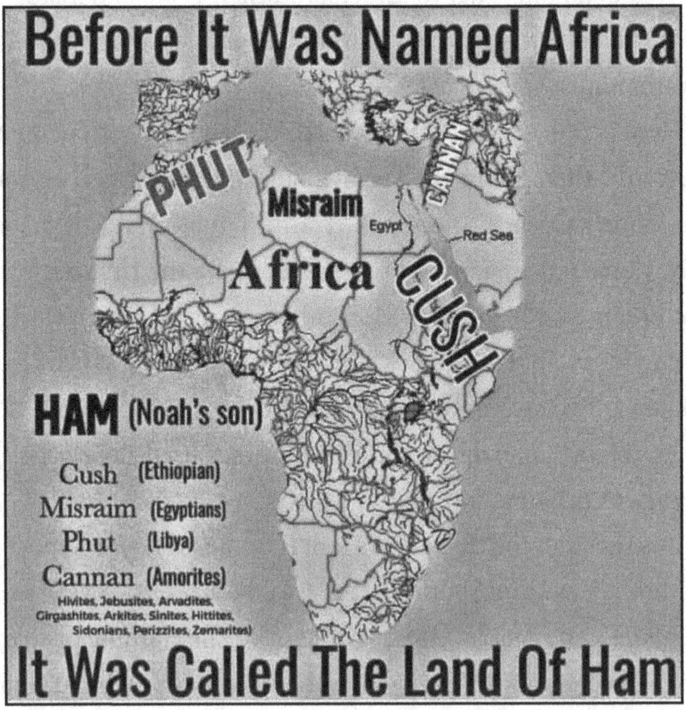

Google Map

Aethiopian or Ethiopian Sea or Ocean was the name given to the southern half of the Atlantic Ocean in classical geographical works. The name appeared in maps from ancient times up to the turn of the 19th century.[15]

As much as reading names, chapter after chapter, can be boring, they and their genealogies are an important source of historical information. Names can develop into well-known ethnonyms (a name applied to a given ethnic group, tribe, or people) and toponyms (names of places) which enable researchers to determine historical and geographical information of importance. By demonstrating Ham's genealogy alone, we can witness his importance both from an ancient historical perspective and the world today. Here are examples.[(16)]

Ham. Also known as *Cham or Kham.* Literal meanings are *passionate, hot, burnt, or dark* (father of the Australoid, Negroid and Mongoloid people groups - *Hamites*). He was the progenitor of:

(1) Canaan, meaning "down low", "that humbles and subdues", (sons were Zidon[1], Heth, Amori, Gergashi, Hivi, Arkee, Seni, Arodi, Zimodi and Chamothi) – also known as *Canaanites, Cana, Chna, Chanani, Chanana, Canaana, Kana, Kenaanah, Kena'ani, Kena'an, Kn'nw, Kyn'nw, Kinnahu, Kinahhi, Kinahni, Kinahna, Kinahne* (father of the Mongols, Asians, Orientals, Chinese, Tibetans, Taiwanese, Thais, Vietnamese, Laotians, Cambodians, Japanese, Eskimos, American Indians, Malayasians, Indonesians, Filipinos, Hawaiians, Maoris, Polynesians, Tahitians, Guamanians, Samoans, Fijians, Tongans, Pacific Islanders and related groups);

(2) Cush, meaning "black" or "dark-skinned" (sons were Nimrod, Seba, Havilah, Sabta, Raama and Satecha) – also known as *Chus, Kush, Kosh, Cushaean* (father of Arabia, Land of Shinar, Ninevah, Cushites, Nubians, Ethiopians, Ghanaians, other Africans groups,

Bushmen, Pygmies, Australian Aborigines, New Guineans, other related groups).

(3) Mizraim, meaning "double straits" (sons were Lud, Anom, Pathros, Chasloth and Chaphtor) - also known as *Misraim, Mitzraim, Mizraite, Mitsrayim* (father of Egyptians, Khemets, Copts, other related groups south of Egypt).

(4) Phut, meaning "a bow" (sons were Gebul, Hadan, Benah and Adan) – also known as *Punt, Puta, Put, Puni, Phoud, Pul, Fula, Putaya, Putiya, Libia, Libya* (father of Libyans, Cyrenacians, Tunisians, Berbers, Somalians, Sudanese, North Africans, other related groups).

3. Cush Son of Ham: The Man and The Land

Cush (or Kush) was Ham's eldest son and a grandson of Noah. The word Cush means black or dark-skinned in Hebrew. He was the brother of Canaan, Mizraim and Phut. Cush was the father of Nimrod, a king called the "first heroic warrior on earth," and also Seba, Havillah, Sabtah, Raamah and Sabtecha; and the grandfather of Sheba and Dedan.[17][18]

Each of the sons, as well as Cush their father, migrated and settled in separate geographical places (locations). For example, Nimrod settled in the Land of Shinar (in today's Iraq) whereas Havilah and his descendants settled in the Southwest and Northeast of the Arabian Peninsula. He and many of his children eventually went South till they finally entered into and spread themselves over the northeast, northwest, southern and central Africa, giving the name of Kush (or Cush) to the land they inhabited which was a large portion of Africa South of Egypt.[19] The Cushitic languages of today are named after Cush.[20]

The Cushitic Languages are an offshoot of the Afro-asiatic language family. This language family consists of about 300 languages that are spoken predominantly in Western Asia, North Africa, the Horn of Africa and parts of the Sahel.[21] With the exception of Semitic Languages, all branches of the Afro-Asiatic family are spoken exclusively on the African continent.[22]

The form *Kush (Cush)* appears in Egyptian records as early as the reign of Mentuhotep II (21st century BCE), in an inscription detailing his campaigns against the Nubian region.[23]

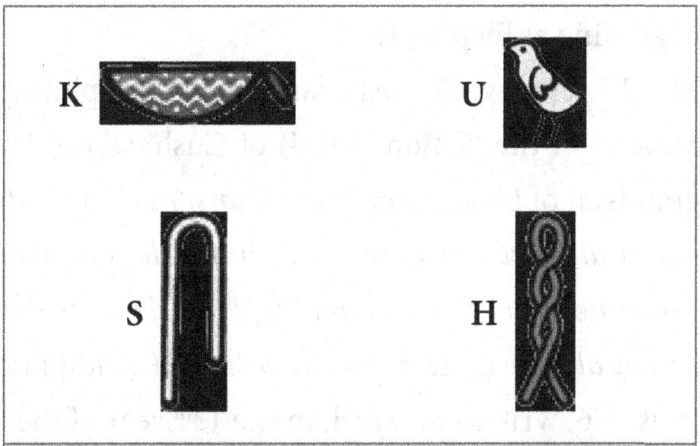

KUSH (or Cush)

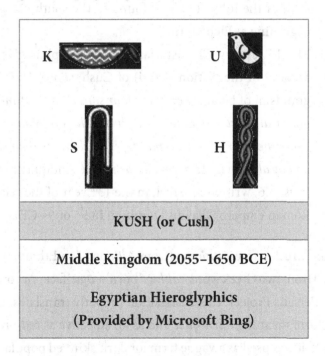

Middle Kingdom (2055–1650 BCE)

Egyptian Hieroglyphics
(Provided by Microsoft Bing)

Historians of the time referred to the area as "The Land of Kush" or the Kingdom of Kush (also spelt Cush) or Ethiopia (when

Ancient Greek influence prevailed in the known world of that era). Here are some important examples:

- Homer (c. 8th century BCE) is the first to have mentioned "Aethiopians" (Ethiopia), writing that they are to be found at the east and west extremities of the world, divided by the sea into "eastern" (at the sunrise) and "western" (at the sunset). Homer was an ancient Greek author and epic poet.[24]
- In his "Histories" (c. 440 BCE, ed. A. D. Godley), Herodotus presents some of the most ancient and detailed information about "Aethiopia" In his view, "Aethiopia" is all of the inhabited land found to the south of Egypt, beginning at Elephantine.
- The 1st century CE historian Flavius Josephus gives an account of the Nation (Land) of Cush, son of Ham and grandson of Noah: "*For of the four sons of Ham, time has not at all hurt the name of Cush; for the Ethiopians over whom he reigned, are even at this day, both by themselves and by all men in Asia, called Cushites*" ("Antiquities of the Jews" 1.6, written in Greek in the 13th year of the reign of Roman emperor Flavius Domitian in 93 or 94 CE).

The Greek name *Aithiopia* (from *Aithíops*, "an Ethiopian") is derived from two Greek words: *aíthiō*, 'burn' + *ṓps*, 'face'. According to the Perseus Project, this designation properly translates into a noun form meaning *burnt-face* and as an adjective as *red-brown*. As such, it was used as a vague term for dark-skinned populations since the time of Homer.[25] The term was applied to such peoples when within the range of observation of the ancient geographers, primarily in what was then Nubia (in ancient Sudan). With the expansion of geographical discoveries and knowledge, the exonym (non-native name) successively extended to other areas below the Sahara.(26)

The translation of Cush (Kush) into Ethiopia found itself elsewhere. Experts have indicated that the Hebrew name of Kush (meaning black or dark-skinned) was eventually translated as Aithiopia in the Septuagint (which is the 3rd century CE Greek translation of the Hebrew Bible and the deuterocanonical books). AEthiopia in the Vulgate Bible (late 4th Century C.E. Bible translation in Latin) was the standard in the western world until the Reformation, and MOHRENDLAND (meaning "negroland" or the country of the blacks) was in the Bible translated in German by Martin Luther and published in 1534 C.E.

With this in mind, the names of Kush and Cushites, of Ethiopia and The Ethiopians have been used interchangeably, depending on whether one spoke Hebrew or Greek, which resulted in these names conveying reference to the Land of Ham or the Land of Kush.(27)

Kush became the representative of the dark race and the term "Ethiopian", the Greek equivalent, was used to designate the same. So, whichever term is employed by ancient writers it means, and has reference, to what is ordinarily called a black man (28)

Paraphrasing J. Pye Smith (1774 - 1851), D.D., F.R.S. in his "Dispersion Of Nations" found in the *Encyclopedia* of that time, he stated: "*The Ethiopians, first on the Arabian side of the Red Sea, then colonizing the African side and subsequently extending indefinitely to the West show that Cushite (Jeremiah 13:23) became the name associated with a dark-skinned person, a black person, a Negro*".(29)

To the thorough scholar or historian, this conclusion strongly indicated that the Cushites and their children were acknowledged to be none other than the descendants of Ham who, therefore, is (among many other ethnic groups) the ancestral head of the Negro ethnic group.

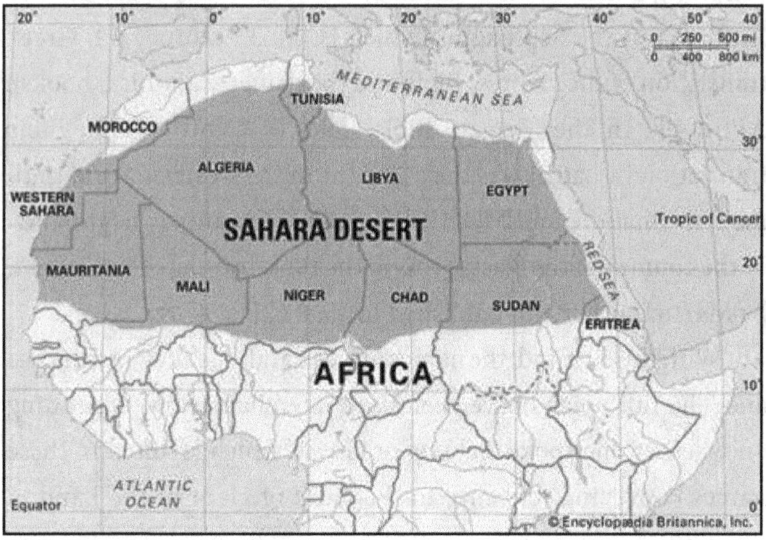

The Sahara Desert is the largest HOTEST desert in the world, and the third largest overall after Antarctica and the Artic. Sub-Sahara is the area of Africa which is south of the Sahara and considered to be inhabited by Blacks or Negroes. For a long time, it was an obstacle to reach the interior of Africa and that is the main reason why Europeans of old called it the Dark Continent (dark for unknown).

Footnote:

1. Location 391, Kindle Edition of "*The Last Hour: An Israeli Insider Looks at the End Times*" by Amir Tsarfati with forward by David Jeremiah, Published by Chosen Books in 2018.
2. Reynolds, Susan (October 1983). "*Medieval Origines Gentiumand the Community of the Realm". History. Chichester, West Sussex: Wiley-Blackwell. 68 (224): 375–390.*
3. Rogers, Jeffrey S. (Year 2000), *p.1271.* *"Table of Nations". In Freedman, David Noel; Myers, Allen C. (eds.). Eerdmans Dictionary of the Bible. Amsterdam University Press.*
4. Kalisch, Marcus M., *A Historical and Critical Commentary of the Old Testament,* London, UK, Longmans, Brown, Green, 1858, p.235.
5. Kautzsch, Prof., quoted by James Orr, "*The Early Narratives of Genesis,*" in The Fundamentals, vol.1, Biola Press, 1917, p.234.
6. Charles F. Pfeifer. The Wycliffe Bible Commentary, Chicago: Moody Press, 1962, p.14.
7. William J. Tinkle, Genetics Favors Creation, "Creation Research Society Quarterly", December 1977, pp155—156.
8. "*Biblical Geography,*" *Catholic Encyclopedia*: "The ethnographical list found in the Bible's Book of Genesis Chapter 10 is a valuable contribution to the knowledge of the old general geography of the East, and its importance can scarcely be overestimated."
9. "*The Table of Nations (Genealogy of Mankind) and the Origin of Nations (History of Man*" by Tim Osterholm, Website: http://www.crystalsoftwaredesign.com/Genealogy/Nations.html
10. Kautzsch, Prof. Emil Friedrich (1841-1910), quoted by James Orr, "The Early Narratives of Genesis," in The Fundamentals, vol.1, Biola Press, 1917, p.234.
11. Bill Cooper, "*The Early History of Man Part 1: The Table of Nations*", EN Tech. J., vol. 4, 1990, p.67.

12. *"The Table of Nations (Genealogy of Mankind) and the Origin of Nations (History of Man"* by Tim Osterholm, Website: http://www.crystalsoftwaredesign.com/Genealogy/Nations.html
13. "Ibid" by Tim Osterholm
14. Evans, William M (February 1980), "*From the Land of Canaan to the Land of Guinea: The Strange Odyssey of the 'Sons of Ham'*", American Historical Review, 85 (1): 15-43
15. 1799 James Rennell map with the Aethiopian Sea in the Gulf of Guinea area.
16. "*The Table of Nations (Genealogy of Mankind) and the Origin of Nations (History of Man)*" by Tim Osterholm, Website: http://www.soundchristian.com/man/, December 2021 Updated
17. *Williams, Frank (2008-11-27). The Panarion of Salamis: Book I (Sections1-46), Second Edition.*
18. *"Genesis 10:8-12". Bible (New Living Translation ed.). Tyndale House. 2006.*
19. "*Early Settlements of the Cushites*", The Cushite, Or The Descendants Of Ham by Rufus Lewis Perry, published in 1893, page 17
20. The Encyclopedia Britannica: A Dictionary of Arts, Sciences, and General Literature, *C. Scribner's Sons. 1878. p. 729.*
21. Robert Hetzron, "Afroasiatic Languages" in Bernard Comrie, The World's Major Languages, 2009, p. 545
22. "*Afro-Asiatic languages*". Encyclopedia Britannica, Published: 25 May 2020
23. The Encyclopedia Britannica: A Dictionary of Arts, Sciences, and General Literature, *C. Scribner's Sons. 1878. p. 729.*
24. Wilson, Nigel (2013). Encyclopedia of Ancient Greece. Routledge. p. 366. 22 November 2016.
25. Fage, John. A History of Africa. Routledge. pp. 25–26. 20 January 2015
26. Liddell, Henry George; Scott, Robert. "Aithiops". A Greek-English Lexicon. Perseus. 2 December 2017.

27. "Early Settlements of the Cushites", The Cushite Or The Descendants Of Ham by Rufus Lewis Perry, published in 1893, page 18
28. "Color of the Egyptians", The Cushite Or The Descendants Of Ham by Rufus Lewis Perry, published in 1893, page 41
29. "Early Settlements of the Cushites", The Cushite Or The Descendants Of Ham by Rufus Lewis Perry, published in 1893, page 21

Chapter III

The Origin of the Name Africa and the Word Negro

As a brief introduction, it is important to note that this chapter is a prolongation of the previous one in that, along with Chapter II entitled "All Came from One Family – Origin of Nations & of Mankind", it establishes a foundation, a basis, for understanding the movement called "La Negritude".

The movement has been known for honoring Black identity and dignity, for emphasizing African cultural heritage, for challenging Eurocentric norms, for promoting self-affirmation, and for recognizing and applying unity among people of African heritage. In essence, it emerged as a response to colonial oppressions in order to regain its racial and ethnic identity.

Today, it is a movement, an ideology you might say, that confirms it was developed as a result of colonialism and a need to re-identify itself with its people, the Blacks or Negroes, as well as with its past roots while, at the same time, incorporating certain values of the former Colonialist that might be beneficial for the continent's development and growth. Therefore, "La Negritude" or "Blackness" evolved from a colonial and post-colonial movement to addressing the concerns of the African people and their future.

It is with this image in mind that we now turn to another two characteristics of the sub-Saharan African, the Negro, in order to understand his or her persona, his or her character. These two characteristics are related to the name Africa and the word Negro. In this respect, the chapter shall explore their origins and meaning, and determine the perceptions that evolved over time in regard to that name and that word. In this way, when combining the information of the previous chapter and this one, a clear description of the persona of the sub-Saran African or Negro is discovered and explained.

A. The Name Africa: The Never Ending Debate

Africa is one of the largest continents in the world (actually the second largest after Asia). So, you would think Africans themselves would have created a name for the continent they lived in. But … they have not … there is no convincing or compelling documentation to point out they have … as we will witness.

The name **Africa** carries a rich history and has sparked countless discussions among scholars, linguists, and historians. Its etymology is a subject of ongoing debate, with various theories vying for prominence. From ancient geographers to modern researchers, everyone has weighed in on the origins of this iconic name.

The origin of the name Africa has been, and still is, the subject of much discussion and deliberation. A prevailing explanation or determination of how Africa was given its name is far from universal – in other words, its origin has been a debatable subject without a definitive conclusion. With this in mind, however, there are several hypotheses and theories that have been developed which merit attention.

This section will briefly identify and cover the most popular hypotheses and then, with more detail, it shall cover the most compelling theories that explain and establish how Africa was given its name.

1. Popular Hypotheses

Etymological hypotheses can be popular among people. However, though they have been assumed to be true, they lack the evidence to confirm their validity - or in our case the validity of the origin of the ancient name "Africa". They are, therefore, suppositions or proposed explanations that in themselves imply insufficient evidence but that are nevertheless popular as they are accepted by or are prevalent among people in general (and therefore of importance).

By etymological we mean relating to the origin and historical development of words and names and their meanings.

Here are a few such popular hypotheses related to the origin of the name Africa, with brief explanations as to their meaning.

- **ALKEBULAN**(1)

  This idea is very popular within black communities who believe that the name of Africa is Alkebulan. The claim is that Alkebulan is the oldest name for Africa and that in Arabic it means "The Land of the Blacks". This could not be accurate because "The Land of the Blacks" in Arabic is "Bilad-as-Sudan". But according to other sources the word Alkebulan means "mother of mankind" or even "garden of Eden".

In addition, some believe that the word "alkebulan" is derived from the Arabic adverb "qabl" meaning "before". "Al" is the definite article "the", and the suffix "lan" denotes the plural form of the adverb. Thus, the Arabic word "alkebulan" means "the ones before", or simply put "the indigenous people". And so, the name has a deep connection to the land and its people. In this sense, Alkebulan symbolizes the ancient roots of the people of that continent.

It is interesting to note, however, that in the explanation provided, the origin of the words (or parts of the word Alkebulan) are of Arabic language origin and not of African language origin.

- **FRIQI and PHARIKA**[(2)]

FRIQI and PHARIKA are intriguing names that have been associated with the ancient name of Africa.

Many experts actually believe that the name Africa came from two Phoenician words. These words are "friqi" and "pharika" which would respectively translate into corn and fruit.

According to this hypothesis, the Phoenicians called Africa "the land of corn and fruit", which would align well with the continents rich agriculture heritage. The Phoenicians inhabited cities along the coast of the Mediterranean, and it is quite possible that they were able to discover at least parts of Africa.

Who were the Phoenicians? Archeology Professor Ephraim Stern identifies the Phoenicians as Canaanites. At its height between 1100 and 200 BCE, Phoenician civilization spanned the Mediterranean from Cyprus to the Iberian Peninsula. Carthage, a settlement in northwest Africa, became a major civilization in its own right in the 7th century BCE

The Phoenicians were a Semitic-speaking people and were renowned among contemporaries as skilled traders and mariners. Their best known legacy is the world's oldest verified alphabet which they invented about 1200 BCE and passed onto the Greeks, and is the basis of the alphabet used today.(2)(3)

- **APHRIKĒ**(3)

The name of the African continent also dealt with its climate. There are those who believe that the name Africa is derived from the Greek word "aphrikē," which denotes a "land that is free from the cold weather and horror". This interpretation brings strong and pleasant images of warmth, vitality, and a place unburdened by hilling elements.

The name finds its roots in "PHRIKE" meaning "cold". So, putting an "a" in front of it would negate it and would mean "not cold". (in effect, the "a" means "no" and so, for example, an atheist is one who has no religion with the "a" meaning "no" and "theist" meaning religion).

The consensus is that "APHRIKE" is not likely to be the original name for Africa.

- **KHAFRE**[(4)]

Other hypotheses have equated "Africa" to the fourth-Dynasty Egyptian pharaoh, Khafre, who ruled from c. 2558 to 2532 BCE. In this respect, some equate Africa with this pharaoh.

The belief is that modern Egyptologists merged ancient Egyptian writing styles and in so doing have mixed up the order of the ancient Egyptian writing style of Kh-afre to mean Afre-Kh or Africa.

2. Compelling Theories

Theories rely on tested and verified data. That is why they are referred to as compelling theories, as opposed to popular hypotheses which are not adequately substantiated.

Therefore, a Compelling Theory involves credible evidence and sources of information which can be vetted and substantiated in order to be believable.

In other words, a "compelling theory" is convincing and accurate when it is based on facts that cannot be disproven – in our case from a historical and geographical point of view because it is being supported in accordance with a set of facts which is based on generally accepted authority (such as ancient and/or contemporary historians and geographers).

Prior to defining the origin of the name Africa from the point of view of Compelling Theory, it is important to mention that, for a good part of human history, Africa went by a totally different name.

Using "Compelling Theory", as an example of credible evidence, it is clear that ancient historians and geographers, such as Herodotus (Greek, referred to as the Father of History, 484-425 BCE) and Strabo (Greek geographer, 63 BCE – 23 CE), actually attributed the name "Libya" to the entire continent – understandably, since from their perspective it was the only world they knew.

Two re-created maps entitled "*The World According to Herodotus, Year 450 BCE*" are shown below. They identify three continents (Europe, Asia, and Libya instead of Africa) as related to the known world of that period. At that time only the Northern end of the African continent had been explored by outsiders, and in today's terms this area comprises the countries of Morocco, Algeria, Tunisia, and modern Libya. It should also be noted that Egypt was not at that time (5th century BCE - Ancient Greece) considered to be a part of the Libya continent (meaning, African) but rather of Asia, with the Nile used as the border between Asia and Africa (then called Libya) – much later, the Red Sea was established as the boundary between Africa and Asia, replacing the Nile.[(5)]

(**Note:** Egypt is considered a transcontinental country because it is located on two continents: Africa and Asia.)

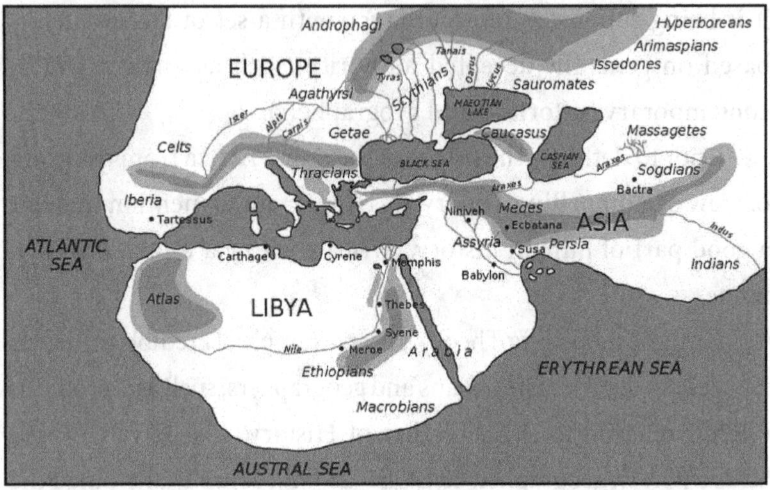

The inhabited world according to Herodotus, the Greek historian and geographer, known as "The Father of History." Published in the World History Encyclopedia April 26, 2012, by Bibi Saint-Pol.

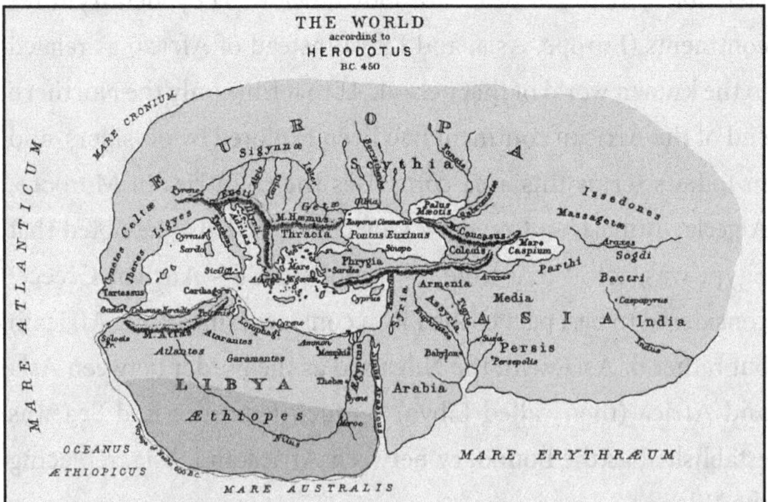

Herodotus World map shaped like a human head. "Human Landscapes and Maps", Panorama of the World, November 26, 2017.

(**Note:** Herodotus traveled in Europe, Asia, and North Africa, gathered information from people he met, and documented his findings in his great treatise Histories, which provides a detailed picture of the cultures of his time. According to his descriptions, the map of the world was also drawn. Greek civilization is at the center of his worldview, his writings and maps, and his narrative is a unified geo-historical.)

This land, consisting of the Northern end of the African Continent, was given the name of "LIBU" by the people who lived to the west of Egypt, and from which the name Libya is derived. For the likes of Herodotus, LIBU came to represent the larger ethnic group of North Africans, which today would be called "Berber" (in other words, the indigenous people of North Africa) and who are lighter skinned and have more western and Arab like features than the Africans further south.[(6)]

To Herodotus there were <u>two ethnicities</u> in Africa: (1) Libyans who were found in the north, and (2) the AEthiopians who were darker skinned people found further south on the continent (this is the original name for Ethiopia which means dark-skinned or black). Nevertheless, Herodotus, and others, called the continent "Libya" to signal that it is the "land of the LIBU".[(6)]

So, what transpired after that? In short, the Romans appeared on the scene.

The Romans, for a long time now at the height of their fame and power, had conquered and controlled the coast of northern Africa. Because it was a large area of land, they established several provinces that included Aegyptus, Cyrenaica, Numidia, and the area around the city of Carthage and modern day Tunisia (which was given the name Africa) – see map below. It then resulted that the name Africa came to mean larger and larger areas until the entire continent was under its title, and the name "Libya" was entirely replaced by "Africa".(7)

Consequently, what we should be asking is "why did the Romans call the province Africa in the first place?"

The ancient Romans would call that area "Africa Terra" which translates from Latin into "land of the Afri". Though it is very likely that the name referred to the Afri people of Northern Africa, the significance and meaning of it all is still being debated as to why they were called Afri.(8)

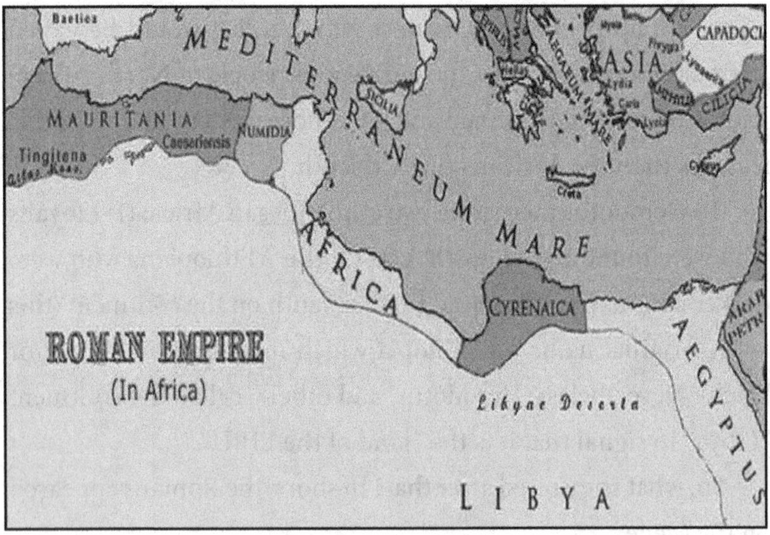

From this debate <u>three main explanations</u> have arisen.

- The first explanation is that "AFRI", or the singular "AFER", came from the Phoenicians who operated throughout the Mediterranean Sea (they emerged on the scene 2,500 BCE, were conquered by the Romans in 64 BCE[9]. In their language the term "AFER" meant "DUST" and could have meant to describe the land where the AFRI lived, which on occasion will experience huge dust and sand storms, sometimes even visible from space.[10]

- The second explanation is that "AFRI" originates from the Berber word "IFRI", meaning "cave" which some people in Tunisia were known to live in, some of whom still do to this day.[11]

  The Berbers are an Afro-Asiatic ethnic group native to North Africa and mostly the Maghreb region of it. Classical Berber Kingdoms existed between 202 BC-698 CE.

- Thirdly, the modern term of Africa, used today in the Western World, most certainly comes from the Romans who called their Northern Province "Africa". To the Romans, the word "Afri" was a Latin term which was largely in reference to all lands south of the Mediterranean Sea. It had been suggested that the "Afri" was a "Libyan or Tunisian Tribe" in the region. Later in history the term Africa began to spread and be used in reference to the whole of the continent: Afri-ca meaning "the land of Afri".[12]

Now, even though our modern understanding of the name Africa predominantly comes from the Romans, there is evidence indicating that the Romans themselves acquired it from somewhere else … in other words, the Romans had help from elsewhere.

The question, however, is: did any civilization in Africa call it "The Continent of Africa?". The answer is yes. It was the Egyptians who first called the continent by the name of Africa. The claim is that Africa is derived from the Egyptian word AF-RUI-KA.[13]

British Egyptologist, Gerald Massey (1828-1907), pointed out that Afru-ika was an Egyptian word which meant "the inner land", "born of" or "birthplace".[14] Here, Massey pointed out the origin of the name Africa. He says, 'The tongue of Egypt tells us that Af-rui-ka is the inner land, born of, or literally the birth-place."

Massey derived an etymology from the Egyptian name ***af-rui-ka***: "*to turn toward the opening of the **Ka**.*" According to him, the ***Ka*** is the energetic double of every person and "*opening of the **Ka***" refers to a womb or birthplace. Therefore, from an ancient Egyptian perspective and meaning, Africa would be "*the birthplace*" (that is, the place of birth of a continent).

This finding of Massey's, as explained above, was published in his work "A Book of The Beginnings", Volume I (1881). It has been cited by numerous scholars over the years, including Dr. Charles Finch, M.D. in his essay entitled "The Works of Gerald Massey: Kamite Origins", in the Journal of African Civilizations (1988).

To conclude, we have the Egyptians themselves telling us that their birthplace was in the inner land of what they called Africa (Af-rui-ka). Is that a coincidence? The fact that the Egyptians were the first to call the continent "Africa" in a way is remarkable. Nevertheless, the debate to determine which theory is absolutely correct (or should I say believable) goes on.

Its etymology is a subject of various theories vying for prominence. From ancient geographers and historians to modern researchers, almost every African expert has weighed in on the origins of this iconic name.

B. The Word Negro: Where Did It Come From?

Bible scholars, theologians, and ethnologists have universally agreed that the Negro ethnic group descended from Ham, son of Noah via the line of Cush (see Genesis 10:6-20).

While it was explained in an earlier section where the Negro (or black person) descended from, we will in this section demonstrate the roots and the meaning of the word that gradually developed from a simple to a complex form of interpretation and understanding (and at times misunderstanding).

However, prior to defining or explaining the roots and the meaning of the word Negro, it is important to show how ethnic groups were created and what motivated the formation of such groups. Bearing in mind that such a subject will create criticism, we must always remember that a prominent ancient Greek philosopher called Aristotle (384-322 BCE) said: "*If you do not wish to be criticized, Do nothing, Say nothing, Be nothing*". Therefore, to do nothing is not an option.

1. Creation of Ethnic Groups – Language Being the Driving Force

In spite of all sorts of secular or conventional views, Mankind (or Humankind as some would prefer) was created with language and therefore with speech. In other words, language did not evolve from grunts, groans, and gurgles but from a meaningful system or method of verbal communication that would allow human beings to speak with each other (and eventually write to each other).

The Cambridge Encyclopedia of Language explains: "*Every culture which has been investigated, no matter how primitive it may be in cultural terms, turns out to have a fully developed language, with a complexity comparable to those of the so-called 'civilized' nation*".[15]

In addition, it is noticeably clear that the Bible categorically supports and confirms that after the Tower of Babel (according to Genesis 11:1-9) the following occurred: **(a)** one language became many, and **(b)** the ethnic groups or nations, that were eventually formed due to languages, were forcibly dispersed.

In other words, at the Tower of Babel, the **Big Bang of Language Diversity** occurred which meant that many languages were brought into existence. This resulted in the formation of groups speaking the same language moving away together as they were forcibly dispersed to fill the earth.

Language diversity, therefore, became the driving force to creating ethnic groups that spoke the same language. In time they developed a common cultural background of beliefs, values, and behaviors, with a common ancestry that is often handed down from one generation to another. Such ethnic groups were the progenitor of tribes, clans, and nations. In addition, the languages they spoke back then have slowly developed into 7,000 plus languages worldwide today, with clear observable and prominent distinctions between the groups (or families) of languages.

Of great importance is that "*linguistic fossils*" or "*fossil words*" do exist and prove the veracity of their ancient linguistic features.[16] Those fossils are a helpful instrument that enable us to research our ancestry. So, what are these fossils, and what do they reveal regarding the origin of human language?

The New Encyclopedia Britannica[17] explains: "*The earliest records of written language, the only linguistic fossils man can hope to have, go back no more than about 4,000 or 5,000 years.*"

Where did archaeologists discover these "linguistic fossils," or "records of written language"?

In lower Mesopotamia (the location of Ancient Shinar, which today is referred to as the Province of Shinar located in present day Iraq), where the Biblical Tower of Babel was built and where ancient cuneiform historical writings were found. Hence, the available physical evidence is in agreement with the facts stated in the Bible.

And, what are linguistic fossils or fossil words? Linguistic fossils are words in a language that are no longer productive or spoken, although they have been preserved in set sentences, phrases, idioms, and in contexts. Like physical fossils, they offer a knowledgeable view of earlier times, throwing light on language from days gone by. Suffice it to say that linguistic fossils and fossil words are a well preserved testimony from time immemorial.[18]

This an example of a clay tablet with cuneiform writing, from Mesopotamia, third millennium B.C.E.

The inscriptions discovered in the past century and a half, have been accurately dated through the advances of archeology. The clay tablet above is just one of very many inscriptions.

2. A Pertinent Qualification Applicable to Understanding the word "Race"

Specifically, of especial and relevant importance is that, prior to the Greek (323 BCE to 146 BCE) and Roman (27 BCE to 395 CE) conquests and dominance of the then known world, people in ancient times did not think of race in the same way we do today. In the century we live in, "race" has tended to be generally defined in terms of skin color and other physical characteristics (as opposed, for example, to being purely impartial towards different shades of color). However, in ancient times, the notion of skin color as the principal reason for designating race did not exist – it would be unfamiliar to those living back then.[19]

Rather, in ancient times, people classified themselves in terms of "ethnicities" or "nationalities".

For example, the Egyptians of antiquity considered themselves as Egyptians and not "black people" or "white people". Likewise, the people belonging to the ancient Kingdom of Kush (or Cush) considered themselves as Kushites (or Cushites), not as "black people". In other words, the peoples of Africa thought of themselves as belonging to a tribe, or ethnic group, or nation and not to a race as defined today … period.[20]

The word "race" interpreted to mean an identifiable group of people who share a common skin color, other physical characteristics and ancestry, was introduced into English in about 1580, from the old French "rasse" (1512).[21] However, the first post Graeco-Roman published classification of humans into distinct races seems to be François Bernier's "*Nouvelle division de la Terre par les Différents Espèces ou Races qui l'Habitent*" (or "New Division of Earth by the Different Species or Races which Inhabit it"), published in 1684.[22]

Categorizing race seems to be a human-invented term used to satisfy describing and classifying people into various social groups based on characteristics like skin color, physical features, and genetic heredity.[22] The ideas of a "white race" or a "black race" or a "yellow race" were invented as concepts based on extremely superficial physical characteristics and are scientifically inappropriate definitions of race. Anthropologists now regard racial divisions as a cultural phenomenon, not a biological one.[23]

At no point, from the first imperfect and crude attempts at

classifying human populations in the 17th and 18th centuries to the present day, have scientists agreed on the number of races of humankind, the features to be used in the identification of races, or the meaning of *race* itself. Experts have suggested a range of different races varying from 3 to more than 60, based on what they have considered distinctive differences in physical characteristics alone (examples include hair type, head shape, skin color, height, and so on). The lack of agreement and cooperation on the meaning and identification of races continued into the 21st century, and contemporary scientists are no closer to agreement than their forebears. Thus, *race* has never had, in the history of its use, a precise meaning.[(24)]

The concept of racial classification schemes provided the most powerful framework for understanding the divide between white, black, and yellow. In referring to the color of skin from a biological concept instead of a nationality or ethnicity undoubtedly enabled the development of scientific racist theories as well as the theory of the so-called Aryan master race. This shall be covered in more detail in the next chapter (chapter IV).

With the classification of "race", from a scientific and biological point of view, differences among humans ceased to form part of "**the belief of a divine and permanent order**", and became part and parcel of an epic struggle for domination. Any analysis that misses this ideological thrust of the race concept will fail to understand why it is that this concept has created so much chaos and affliction.

3. Where Did The Word Negro Come From?

Black is obviously, the English name given to this color. Its origin and its development into the English and other European languages stretches back to a group of tribes known as the Proto-Indo-Europeans (3400 – 2000 BCE).[25] According to etymologists, these ancient groups used the unattractive sounding word BHLEG to mean "burnt, dark, gleam", which eventually developed into the English word "black".[26]

"Black" is a special color. It is attributed to the total absence of all colors which, consequently, lacks brightness; and, although it absorbs light, it does not reflect any back. From a sophisticated quality to a quality manifested in evil, few colors evoke strong positive or negative images as does the color known as "black".

It is often used symbolically or figuratively to represent darkness. Black and white have often been used to describe opposites such as good and evil, the Dark Ages[27] versus the Age of Enlightenment,[28] and night versus day. Since the Middle Ages, black has also been the symbolic color of solemnity and authority, and for this reason judges and magistrates still commonly wear black robes.[29]

Black was one of the first colors used artistically in cave paintings some 5,000 years ago. It was also used by the ancient Egyptians, where black had positive associations as it was the color of fertility and of the rich black soil flooded by the Nile. To ancient Greeks, black represented the underworld, separated from the living by the river Acheron (Greece) whose water ran black (the underworld was the supernatural world of the dead in various religious traditions and myths).[30] To the Roman Empire, it became the color of mourning, and over the centuries it was frequently associated with death, evil, witches, and magic. In the 14th century, clothes made in black were worn by royalty, clergy, judges, and government officials in much of Europe. Today, according to surveys in Europe and North America, it is the color most commonly associated with mourning, the end, secrets, magic, force, violence, evil and elegance.[31] And on it goes.

With this brief background in mind, for just the color "black", we realize that for most of mankind's history people had a deep and thorough understanding of color - including defining each one.

Why is it important to briefly explain the roots of the word black? Simply, because by identifying and defining this color, it allows for a better understanding of what black means and how people perceived it (as for example, either as a common and favorable benefit or as an offending and demeaning one).

Moreover, it helps us, as well, to understand how the word "negro" historically came about and why it was initially referred to as simply the color "black" in a language other than English, which was then transformed to a definition related to ethnicity and nationality, and then different shades of skin color, leading to the creation of races (including the Negroid race)[32], based on biological rather than cultural phenomenon – see previous section entitled "A Pertinent Qualification Applicable to Understanding Race" for more details.

The **origin of the word negro** evolved from the ancient names of Kush (Cush) and Aethiopia (not Canaan or other sons of Ham). The former meant black in Hebrew and the latter also meant black but in the Greek language (actually koine Greek). Cush settled in

East Africa where the name was identified with a kingdom and later with African tribal entities, with the Cushite language being the language of many of those tribes.

When the ancient Greeks later occupied the part of Africa which was known as the Land of Kush (Cush) they started to call the land by their Greek name for black which is Aethiopia or Ethiopia – today it is the name of a country in the eastern part of Africa which was about the only one on the African Continent that remained independent during the European Colonial Era. (See the section entitled "Cush Son of Ham: The Man and The Land").

As the Romans occupied Africa beginning in 146 BCE, they set about differentiating between the northern Africans who were of lighter skin color and the southern Africans, those south of the Sahara Desert, with a darker skin color. In addition, the Romans' official languages were Latin and Greek. Latin was the original language of Romans and remained the language of imperial administration, the military, and legislation throughout the classical period of antiquity (776 BCE and 476 CE).[33]

In time, Latin developed locally in the Empire's Western provinces into a subgroup within what is known as the Indo-European Family of Languages. This subgroup became known as the Romance languages (less commonly known as Latin languages) that included Spanish, Catalan, Portuguese, French, Italian, and Romanian. Also, Latin became the language of conquered areas because people started speaking it; and not because it was imposed on peoples brought under Roman rule.[34]

Latin itself remained an international medium of expression for diplomacy and for intellectual developments identified with

Renaissance humanism up until the 17th century, and for law and the Roman Catholic Church to the present.[35]

Worthy of note is that the age of modern colonialism began about the 15th century CE following the European discoveries of a sea route around Africa's southern coast in 1488 and of America in 1492. With these events, sea power shifted from the Mediterranean to the Atlantic and to the emerging nation states of Portugal, Spain, the Dutch, France, and England. By discovery, conquest, and settlement, these nations expanded and colonized much of the world spreading European institutions and culture.[36] The "Scramble for Africa" and for the "New World" by European countries had officially started, though the policy of colonization was being implemented in the 1880's.

In fact, around 1442, the Portuguese first arrived in Southern Africa while trying to find a sea route to India.[37] The term *negro*, literally meaning "black", was used by the Spanish and Portuguese as a simple description, to refer to the Bantu peoples,[38] that they encountered. *Negro* denotes "black" in Spanish and Portuguese, and is believed to be derived from the Latin word *niger*, meaning *black* (which, as previously noted, is from a Proto-Indo-European Root). "Negro" was also used to identify peoples of West Africa - ancient maps labelled the area Negroland, which stretched along the Niger River. From the 18th century to the late 1960s, *negro* (later capitalized) was considered to be the proper English language term for people of black African origin.[39]

A 1729 map titled: "NEGROLAND and GUINEA, with the European settlements" By Herman Moll (1654-1732) who was a London geographer, cartographer, and engraver.

With the advent of European colonialism, the Romance languages of France, Belgium, Italy, Portugal, and Spain, continued their linguistic influence on local languages where Latin had left off. This is why many names and words in Africa are of Latin origin which, obviously, includes the names Negro to mean a black person, and Negroid meaning a person of black resemblance (the suffix "-oid" actually means similar to).

To conclude, it is a fact that the word negro (which initially simply identified a color) became associated with people whose skin color is black. It is another fact that the name Negroid translates as "black resemblance" as it is derived from the word

Negro or black. In modern usage, Negroid is associated with populations which on the whole possess typical Negro physical characteristics.[40] Finally, it is a proven fact that both Negro and Negroid are of Latin and Ancient Greek etymological roots.[41] All of which indicates that the origin and development of these two words and their meaning are strongly linked historically to the ethnicity (or race, as some would prefer to call it) of those inhabitants living in the southern part of Africa (that is, those inhabiting the lands south of the Sahara Desert).

Footnote:

1. "How Did Africa Get Its Name?", African History Videos, Video No. One, at 1 minute 31 seconds, Website:: www.patreon.com/HomeTeamHistory, 2018 production.
2. "What Was The Original Name Of Africa?", World Atlas, website: www.worldatlas.com dated June 16, 2020
3. "Who Were the Phoenicians?" by Megan Sauter, Biblical Archaeology Society, October 3, 2021, Website: https://www.biblicalarchaeology.org
4. "*How did Africa really get its name*?" by Mildred Europa Taylor, F2Fafrica.com/History, June 24, 2018
5. *Lewis, Martin W.; Wigen, Kären (1997). The myth of continents: a critique of meta- geography. Berkeley and Los Angeles: University of California Press. Lewis & Wigen 1997, pp. 170-173.*
6. Zimmermann, K. (2008). 'Lebou/Libou'. Encyclopédie Berbère. 28-29 | Kirtēsii–Lutte. Aix-en-Provence: Edi Sud, pp. 4361–4363.
7. Herodotus Histories III.114 English translation by A. D. Godley. Cambridge. Harvard University Press. 1920
8. "*How Africa Got Its Name*", African History Videos, Video No. Two, at 1 minute and 15 seconds, Website:: www.patreon.com/HomeTeamHistory, 2018 production.

9. Ibid, Video No. Two, at 2 minutes and 57 seconds
10. **Punic Wars** were a series of conflicts fought between the forces of ancient Carthage and Rome. The main cause of the Punic Wars was the clash of interests between the existing Carthaginian Empire and the expanding Roman Republic. Result: Roman victory, destruction of Carthage.
11. *"Phoenicia Defined"* by Joshua J. Mark, published March 19, 2018, in World History Encyclopedia, Website: https://www.worldhistory.org/phoenicia/
12. George Babington Michell, "*The Berbers*", *Journal of the Royal African Society*, Vol. 2, No. 6 (January 1903), pp. 161-194
13. "*How Africa Got Its Name*", African History Videos, Video No. Two, at 2 minutes and 13 seconds, Website:: www.patreon.com/HomeTeamHistory, 2018 production.
14. "*How Did Africa Get Its Name*", African History Videos, Video No. One, at 4 minutes and 17 seconds, Website: www.patreon.com/HomeTeamHistory, 2018 production
15. The Cambridge Encyclopedia of Language, Cambridge University Press; 3rd edition (July 26, 2010), Principal Author: David Crystal, honorary professor of linguistics at the University of Wales, OBE, FBA, FLSW, FCIL is a British linguist, academic, and author.
16. 1993 (Second Edition, 1989 ed.). Oxford English Dictionary.
17. Britannica Online, "Language: Characteristics of Language: Historical Attitudes Toward Language," at www.britannica.com/topic/language, By Robert Henry Robins, Published: July 26, 1999 and Updated: December 17, 2021
18. The general explanation is from the 22nd edition of Ethnologue, a database covering a majority of the world's population, detailing approximately **7,111** living languages in existence today. Gary Simons | February 21, 2019
19. "Making the Distant Past Relevant to the Present Day: Were the Ancient Egyptians Black?", By Spencer McDaniel, April 23, 2020. Website: https://talesoftimesforgotten.com/2020/04/23/were-the-ancient-egyptians-black/.

20. Ibid, By Spencer McDaniel
21. "Online Etymology Dictionary", Douglas Harper, 2008.
22. Yudell, M.; Roberts, D.; DeSalle, R.; Tishkoff, S., "Taking Race Out Of Human Genetics" (5 February 2016).
23. "Historical Foundations of Race" by David R. Roediger, National Museum of African American History and Culture, Website: https://nmaahc.si.edu/learn/talking-about-race/topics/historical-foundations-race
24. Barnshaw, John (2008). "Race" In Schaefer, Richard T. (ed.). *Encyclopedia of Race, Ethnicity, and Society, Volume 1.* SAGE Publications. pp. 1091–3
25. Race | Definition, Ideologies, Constructions, & Facts | Britannica, https://www.britannica.com/topic/race-human
26. Powell, Eric A., "Telling Tales in Proto-Indo-European", Archeology, Retrieved 30 July 2017 Michel Pastoureau, *Noir – Histoire d'une couleur,* Publisher LE SEUIL, pp 34-39.
27. Pastoureau, Michael (2008). *Black: The History of a Color.* Princeton University Press. p. 216
28. The "**Dark Ages**" is a term that refers to the period between the fall of the Roman Empire and the Renaissance when most of Europe was in decline – 5th to the 12th centuries CE. This period was known as the Dark Ages because it was marked by political regression as well as economic, intellectual, and cultural decline. Whereas the "Renaissance" (a French word meaning Rebirth) covers the 15th and 16th centuries CE, and is characterized by an effort to revive and surpass ideas and achievements of classical antiquity in the areas affecting the art, architecture, philosophy, literature, music, science, technology, politics, religion.
29. The "**Age of Enlightenment**" (also known as the Age of Reason) is the period of Western European intellectual history from the late 17th to the late 18th centuries which advocated such ideals as liberty, progress, tolerance, fraternity, constitutional government, and separation of church and state.

30. Heller, Eva (2009). *Psychologie de la couleur – Effets et symboliques.* Pyramyd (French translation), pp. 105–26
31. Zuffi, Stefano (2012). *Color in Art*, page 270, Publisher: Abrams (June 1, 2012)
32. St. Clair, Kassia (2016). *The Secret Lives of Colour.* London: John Murray. pp. 261-262.
33. "Negroid" has traditionally been used within physical anthropology to denote one of the three declared races of Mankind (or as some would prefer humankind), along side Caucasoid, and Mongoloid. The concept of dividing humankind into three races called Caucasoid, Mongoloid, and Negroid was introduced in the 1780s by members of the Gottingen School of History (Germany) and further developed by Western scholars in the context of racist ideologies during the age of colonialism.
34. Edited by James Clackson, *Introduction To A Companion to the Latin Language*, p. 1, Publisher Name: Wiley-Blackwell; first edition (September 6, 2011).
35. József Herman, *Vulgar Latin*, translated by Roger Wright (Pennsylvania State University Press, 2000, originally published 1975 in French), p. 10
36. Rochette, "Language Policies in the Roman Republic and Empire," p. 549; Charles Freeman, *The Greek Achievement: The Foundation of the Western World* (New York: Penguin, 1999), pp. 389–433.
37. "*Western Colonialism*" by Harry Magdoff, Britannica, 2021 Edition.
38. *Thatcher, Oliver. "Vasco da Gamma: Round Africa to India, 1487-1498 CE". Modern History Sourcebook. Milwaukee: University Research Extension Co. February 19, 2018.*
39. Based on The Greenwood Dictionary of World History, published by the Greenwood Publishing Group (2006). The Bantu people are the speakers of Bantu languages, comprising several hundred indigenous ethnic groups in Africa, spread over a vast area from Central Africa to Southeast Africa, and to Southern Africa. Depending on the definition of language or dialect, it is estimated that there are between 440 and 680 distinct languages in the Bantu grouping.

40. *Mann, Stuart E. (1984). An Indo-European Comparative Dictionary. Hamburg: Helmut Buske Verlag. p. 858.*
41. Founder and Editor: Douglas Harper (November 2001). "*Online Etymological Dictionary*". Etymological means relating to the origin and historical development of words and their meaning.

Chapter IV

Highlighting Definite Aspects of Pre-Colonial Sub-Sahara Africa

A. Introduction to this Chapter

This chapter is about Black Africans, or more specifically the indigenous population referred to as Negroid Ethnic Group, in the context of the geographical area called Sub-Sahara Africa – the area they originally come from.

It is, the ethnic group that probably suffered the most because of the following issues: of race, of slavery, of colonial occupation, of disintegration of the African system of governance which was replaced by hard to understand western European norms and institutions, and of the colonialists' imposition and creation of artificial boundaries that formed new African countries or states south of the Sahara.

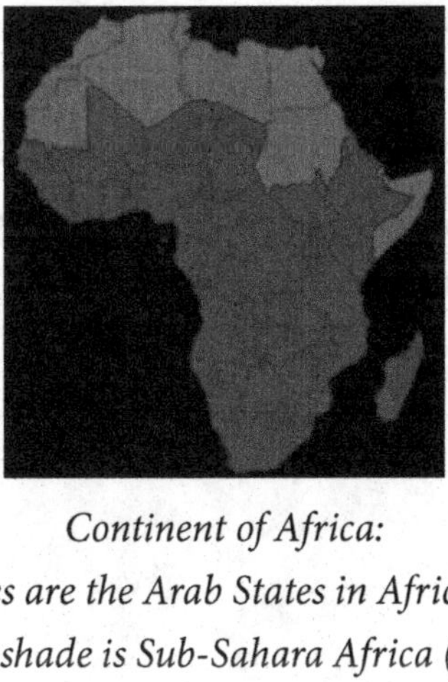

Continent of Africa:
The lighter shades are the Arab States in Africa (Arab League); the darker shade is Sub-Sahara Africa (UNESCO)

We know that the traditional Negro-African society was transformed into a modern society so different from the old one that many expressed a loss of identity culturally, politically, and economically. In addition, artificial boundaries of the newly formed countries created by the colonialists totally disregarded ethnic, tribal, and parochial units which, in many instances, eventually created ethnic tensions that went as far as causing civil wars and tribal ethnic cleansing. It is a fact that there are very few ethnic groups (or races, as some would prefer to call them) that have experienced the same extent of adversity than the Negro of Sub-Saharan Africa.

While the Pre-Colonial Era of Sub-Saharan Africa covers a wide range of historical issues or events such as the Tribal system of governance, Negroid kingdoms, the beginning of migrants from the Arabian Peninsula as well as Europe, there are **three specific pre-colonial issues or events** that had a significant and adverse effect on the persona of the Negro, and his or her living environment, that require to be covered in order to understand and appreciate the predicament of what the Negroid ethnic group eventually had to face.

The three key issues or events helping to understand the predicament of the Negro specifically, and Sub-Sahara Africa in general, and why "La Négritude" developed into a movement directly related to one's skin color and Negroid characteristics, are the issues (1) of race, (2) of slavery, and (3) of colonialism which occurred from pre-colonial times and which continued into the colonial era.

However, prior to covering these three specific issues in some detail, it is important to briefly define certain words and answer certain questions. In doing so, it will be possible to better comprehend and appreciate these three issues of that period of time (race, slavery, colonialism), as well as the post-colonial eras. In this respect, the following will be covered as part of this introductory narrative:

1. What is the meaning of pre-colonial Africa? How is it defined?
2. What is the connection between 9th century C.E. Moslem Spain and the Slavs?
3. How is the word ethnicity defined? How Important Is It In Regard to One's identity?

1. What Is The Meaning Of Pre-Colonial Africa? How Is It Defined?

The "pre-colonial era" means the period prior to the conquest of Africa by European Colonialists. The **Sub-Saharan age of pre-colonial civilization** started in 650 CE and lasted until 1880 CE as shown in the chart below. It was an era, you might say, that comprised three types of civilizations flourishing across Africa: **(a)** the Christian (Ethiopia and medieval Nubia), **(b)** the Islamic kingdoms across the northern half of Africa as well as east coast city-states, and **(c)** the traditional kingdoms across the southern half of Africa ("traditional" in the sense of believing in established indigenous religions and culture).[1]

Throughout most of Sub-Saharan Africa, **urban life** did not emerge until the medieval period; Nubia and Ethiopia are the two exceptions. While ancient Sub-Saharan Africa (2000 BCE-500 CE) was almost bare of cities, the period ca. 650 CE-1880 CE (medieval period) featured a rich variety of civilizations.[1]

Sub-Saharan Africa roughly consists of **black Africa or the Negroid ethnic group**, whereas the indigenous populations of North Africa are the lighter-skinned **Berbers** (throughout the Maghreb) and **Egyptians** (in Egypt). Following the expansion of the Islamic Caliphate, North Africa was heavily settled by **Arabs** who mixed and interacted with native peoples.[2]

Summary of the History of Sub-Saharan Africa

ca. 2000-1000 BC early Nubian civilization	Nubian civilization lives in the shadow of Egypt
ca. 1000 BC-300 CE Kush (Cush)	Nubia flourishes as the independent kingdom of Kush and spreads to other parts of Africa
ca. 300-650 CE Aksum (modern day Ethiopia & Eritrea)	The kingdom of Aksum experiences the peak of its power (ca. 300, Aksum achieves regional dominance by destroying Kush; ca. 650, Aksum declines as Islamic civilization spreads across northern Africa)

ca. 650-1880 CE age of pre-colonial civilizations	Three types of civilizations flourish across Africa: **Christian** (Ethiopia and medieval Nubia), **Islamic** (kingdoms across the northern half of Africa, as well as east coast city-states), and **Traditional** (kingdoms across the southern half of Africa)
ca. 1880-1980 CE colonial Africa	European powers (predominantly Britain and France) seize and govern Africa
ca. 1980 CE to present (modern day Africa)	Generally, the era in which modern independent countries, in Sub-Saharan Africa, created mainly by European colonialists (during the colonial era), regardless of tribal affiliations, are now governed by indigenous leaders.

Brief History of Sub-Saharan Africa | Essential Humanities (essential-humanities.net)

Today, the population of sub-Saharan Africa is growing and according to Global Trends in 2018 the population was approximately 1.1 billion of which the religion of Christianity formed 62.9%, Islam 30.2%, and the Traditional faiths 3.3% primarily consisting of Animism which includes various aspects of polytheistic and pantheistic beliefs.[3]

As can be appreciated from the history of Sub-Saharan Africa in Pre-Colonial times, the continent consisted of tribal kingdoms and of a civilization of a relatively high level of cultural and archeological advancements portrayed in their writing system and the keeping of written records.

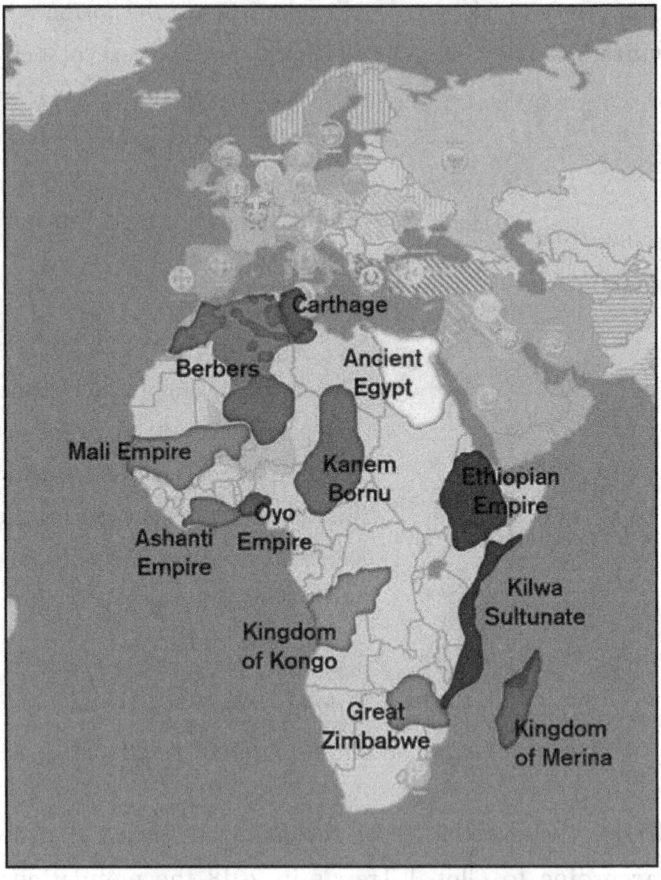

Pre-Colonial Africa: African Civilizations

Examples of prominent Pre-Colonial African Civilizations are the following:

- **Egypt**: Known for its monumental pyramids, pharaohs, and the Nile River civilization.

- **Nubia**: Flourished along the Nile, with impressive architecture and cultural achievements.
- **Ghana**: A powerful trading empire in West Africa.
- **The Berbers**: A medieval empire that flourished as a center of culture and trade in North Africa.
- **Mali**: Known for its wealth, gold trade, and the legendary ruler Mansa Musa.
- **Carthage**: A maritime civilization in North Africa.
- **Zimbabwe**: Home to the complex Great Zimbabwe civilization.
- **Kongo (or Congo)**: Flourished in Central Africa.
- **Ashanti Empire**: A sophisticated empire in West Africa.
- **Sudan**, **Songhai**, and **Gao**: Flourished in West Africa.
- **Aksum**: An ancient kingdom in the Horn of Africa.

In summary, civilization encompasses both material progress and cultural sophistication, shaping the way societies function and interact with one another. Whether ancient or modern, civilizations leave a lasting impact on humanity's collective journey through time.

The geography of Africa helped to shape the history and development of the culture and civilizations of Ancient Africa. The geography impacted where people could live, important trade resources such as gold and salt, and trade routes that helped different civilizations to interact and develop.(4)

2. Where Does The Word Slave Come From? What is the Connection Between 9th Century C.E. Moslem Spain and the Slavs?

Evidence of slavery predates written records, and its practice has existed in almost every ancient civilization. For example: slavery occurred in civilizations as old as Sumer (c. 4000 BCE), Ancient Egypt (c. 3100 BCE), Nubia (2500 BCE), Assyria (c. 2100 BCE), Babylon (c.1894 BCE), Ancient China (c. from 1800s' BCE), Ancient Greece (c. 1200 BCE), the Roman Empire (from 30 BCE), the Arab Islamic Caliphate and Sultanate (from 632 CE), etc.(5)

Ancient slavery consisted of different types of enslavements. It was a mix: from what they called debt-slavery, punishment for crimes, spoils of war, prisoners of war, children born to slaves, serfdom, to outright ownership or property – the last type meant that the person was completely deprived of any rights given to free persons.(6)

The etymology of the word slave goes back to the time of the Muslim occupation of Spain which started in 711 C.E. and ended in 1492 C.E.

The word Slav is attributed to the peoples who inhabited central and east Europe. Many were historically reduced to the state of slavery by the Muslims of Spain during the 9th century C.E. as suggested by **Earnest Klein** (born in Hungary in 1899, and died in 1983 in Canada, who was a linguist, author, and a rabbi).(7)

As Slavs arrived in Muslim-occupied Spain they were subdivided into two groups: **one** consisted of the slaves of Slavic origin who were recognized as a highly valued commodity, and

the other were Slavic warriors who became mercenaries in the service of the Arabic rulers of Spain.

The Slavic slaves in the possession of Muslim Spain included **female** concubines for the harems of the rich Arabs, who were especially valued for their light complexion and blonde hair, and **males**, often brought in as young boys, who either became civil servants, palace servants, eunuchs at the harems, or, in the case of the physically strongest specimen, troops of the elite *Slavic Guards*, serving as "praetorian guards," whose soldiers enjoyed special privileges from the Arabic rulers of Spain.

Arab Slave Market of White Females by David Roberts (well-known lithograph expert 1796-1864)

Spoils of war 19th century C.E. Sheikh looks at the war profit: a woman. Credit: clu. Getty Images no. 1036922048.

It must also be added that part of the Slavic slaves who arrived in Spain were later transferred to other locations in the Muslim world, like North Africa and the Middle East. The Slavic slaves were originally brought to Muslim Spain via Galicia, Frankia, the Lombard Kingdom, and Calabria in Southern Italy.

The Slavs arrived in Muslim Spain quite early on. Already in 762 C.E. we learn of a certain Arabic diplomat named Abd ar-Rahman al-Fihri, who arrived from the East to battle on behalf of the Abbasids (a caliphate name, who ruled from 750 to 1258 C.E.), who had the nickname of ***as-Saqlabi*** (the Slav) because he was tall, had auburn hair and blue eyes. There were also many Slavs at the court of the Omayyad Emir of Cordoba al-Hakam I (796-822).[(8)]

It is from this perspective that it is strongly believed that the English term slave had its origins, its roots, in the word slav.[9]

As the word evolved, it was determined that the European words *Slav* and *slave* developed from the Medieval Latin *sclavus* (c. 900 CE). The English word slave first appears in English around 1290 C.E., and at the time it was spelt sclave. This spelling is based on Old French esclave from Medieval Latin sclavus, The word Sclavus comes from Byzantine Greek sklabos which appears around 600 C.E.[10]

As Slavs were captured and enslaved (because of medieval wars) it led to the word slav becoming synonymous to "**enslaved person**"..... according to this version, the self-name of the Slavs and their Modern Greek name coincided phonetically purely by chance.[10]

Further, the ancient Romans used the Latin word **servus** for "slave." This Latin word is the ancestor of our word servant. In French, servus became serf and was used for a slave who belonged to a piece of land rather than to an individual.[10]

It is important to note that Slavic languages spoken today belong to the Indo-European family. Customarily, Slavs today are subdivided into East Slavs (chiefly Russians, Ukrainians, and Belarusians), West Slavs (chiefly Poles, Czechs, Slovaks, and Wends, or Sorbs), and South Slavs (chiefly Serbs, Croats, Bosnians, Slovenes, Macedonians, and Montenegrins).[11]

3. How is the word ethnicity defined? How Important Is It In Regard to One's identity?

Ethnicity. Identity. These are two of many concepts (others being, for instance, nationality and race) that can bring people together, as much as they are also concepts that can divide people. At an extreme, they can in fact destroy people. Many tribal wars have started because of ethnicity whereby ethnic groups with different values have not been able to live together in the same communal system of governance or because an ethnic group had been looked upon as inferior to others resulting in its subjugation.

Therefore, ethnicity can either be an instrument of social transformation or a weapon of discrimination, depending upon the circumstances existing in a given society. It could create the conditions of cohesion or division (as for example, changes in social structures and institutions, changes in values and norms, changes in population or demographic mix, economic and political change, OR conflicts related to tribal issues, cultural change, social movements).

Different ethnicities linking hands in a concept of caring and acceptance. PublicDomain

However, regardless of how one perceives these concepts, the fact of the matter is that they have influenced the past, they continue to influence the present, and they certainly have the potential to influence the future.

For the sake of understanding ethnicity and identity, it is crucial or vital to remember that the creation of language was the driving force in the eventual formation of ethnic groups, followed by peoples with different physical characteristics, and then nations. That happened when (a) the Big Bang of Language Diversity occurred - at the Tower of Babel - which formally caused the establishment of groups, each with a common and different speech; (b) with every group with a common speech eventually dispersing and migrating to different geographical areas to fill the earth; and (c) as they settled in different geographical areas and remained isolated from each other over long periods of time, they developed different physical characteristic in order to adapt to their environment. These developments marked the origin of ethnic groups and the eventual creation of nations on earth based on different physical characteristics.

In this context, how can the word ethnicity be defined, and how Important is it in regard to developing an identity?

The term **"ethnicity"** has compelling linguistic history. It has its roots in Ancient Greek and found its way into Latin. It is derived from the Greek word "ethnos" and "ethnikos" which essentially means a collective of humans and is often understood as "people" or "nations" in addition to racial origin, culture, shared ancestry, traditions, language. In another words, it is a group of people who identify with each other based on shared attributes that distinguish them from other groups.[(12)]

From the Greek *ethnikos* and the Latin *ethnicus,* the term ethnicity entered the English language in the mid-1700s.[13]

Ethnicity plays a significant role in shaping an individual's identity. **Identity** has many sides and shades to it. It includes how a person or group perceives itself and how others (outsiders) perceive a person or group. It enables the development of a sense of self, values, and worldview. Therefore, belonging to a specific ethnic group provides a sense of identity and belonging – a sense of community. It helps individuals understand their roots, heritage, traditions, and cultural practices, and tends to fosters pride and strengthens identity.[14]

In summary, ethnicity significantly influences identity by shaping cultural practices, providing a sense of belonging and awareness, and impacting how we perceive ourselves and others. Remember that identities are multifaceted (has many sides and shades), and understanding the interplay between race, ethnicity, and culture enriches self-awareness and empathy.

Therefore, ethnicity significantly impacts on how people construct their identities as it creates a set of traits that distinguishes one group from another (or an individual from another) and ultimately provides a sense of security and continuity.

B. The Sin of Ham and the Curse on His Son Canaan - What is the Meaning of this Sin and Curse? and Why the Intentional Misinterpretation by Some In Regard to the Negro Ethnic Group?

It is universally agreed by Bible scholars, theologians, and ethnologists that the Negro ethnic group or race descended from Ham (via Cush his son).

While it is generally admitted that the black race or Negroes descended from Ham, it is also claimed that Noah put a curse upon Canaan, one of Ham's sons and that therefore his descendants (or the Negro race) are divinely cursed and are inferior to other races. This is a grave mistake. The Bible does not sustain such a theory. The Negro race is just as fully blessed by God as all of the races and ethnicities related to mankind.[15]

So, what is behind this shocking story, a story that falsely accuses and denies a people their full right as equals to any other ethnicity or race? Did not God create all of mankind, without exception, in His image, in His spirit?

Long ago, in those days, finding someone naked (uncovered) was shameful, it was a cultural taboo (as when Adam and Eve, because of their sin, felt shame at their own nakedness (Genesis 3:6-7). This act would be as bad as linking a person to sexual sin, perversion, or dishonor today.

In regard to Noah, the story in Genesis chapter 9 states that he planted a vineyard and made wine from the grapes. He then drank the wine, became drunk, and passed out naked in his tent (Genesis

9:20-21). His son Ham entered the tent, saw his father's nakedness, and went to tell his brothers (Genesis 9:22). Whatever Ham did by discovering his father's nakedness was wicked enough to invite Noah's wrath when he sobered up. Noah then pronounced a strong curse on Canaan, Ham's son (Genesis 9:24).

Sin of Ham and Curse of Canaan (Source: Microsoft Bing)

Noah's Curse on Canaan, Ham's Son. Credit: ZU_09. Getty Images no.1497411532.

According to Donald Lee Stewart, an American minister and preacher, one of the most successful Christian writers in the USA on subjects related to proof or evidence for the Christian faith, Ham innocently came upon his father, after he had unconsciously uncovered himself because of being drunk. The sin of Ham is that he told his brothers of what he had seen. In doing so it brought shame to the entire family. The culture in which this event occurred considered it a crime. In the ancient world, merely seeing one's father naked was a highly offensive act.

As Noah's story unfolded, when Noah sobered up and came to, he discovered what had happened and leveled a curse on Canaan, one of Ham's sons. He said: "*Cursed be Canaan! The lowest of slaves will he be to his brothers*" (Genesis 9:25).

The "curse" on Canaan is more of a prophecy. Noah learned of Ham's sin and gave him the bad news that one line of his descendants would suffer. As a prophet of God, Noah foresaw that the Canaanites, in their wickedness, would deserve their fate (See Leviticus chapter 18 for a list of future Canaanite sins). Ham's punishment was the absence of a fatherly blessing and to know that he was the ancestor of a doomed people group, the Canaanites.(16)

Noah's curse and the prophecy that followed came true during the time of Joshua. The Canaanites, descendants of Ham, were conquered by the Israelites who are descendants of Shem. True to God's Word, some of the Canaanites became slaves (Joshua 9:27 and 17:12-13).(17)

The inclusion of this shameful incident in the life of Noah is interesting. Out of all that Noah did after the flood, why is this episode the only one recorded? The answer lies in the events surrounding the writing of Genesis. Moses, the author of Genesis, was leading the Israelites toward the Land of Canaan to take possession of it. The story of how Canaan came to be cursed was one justification for the conquest of that land by the Israelites. God had pronounced doom upon these people long ago, and it was time for that prophecy to be fulfilled.[18]

Those who adhere to the theory that black or dark-skinned people are cursed have pointed to the fact that Ham's descendants include Africans (blacks). They also say Ham's name, which means "*passionate, hot, burnt, or dark*" in Hebrew, is evidence that the dark-skinned people of the world, who mostly come from warmer climates, are all Ham's children and therefore part of the curse on Ham's son Canaan. This includes Cush (or Kush), Ham's other son, whose name means ""*black*" or "*dark-skinned*" and settled in the eastern part of Africa, and who had nothing to do with what happened in Noah's tent.[19]

Invoking or citing the "sin of Ham and the curse of Canaan" was a tactic developed at the start of the enslavement of the Negro by Europeans in the 17th century C.E., culminating with the rise of the Atlantic slave trade, in an effort to justify forced racial-based slavery.[20]

Talk of the "sin of Ham and the curse of Canaan" was especially prevalent in the United States in the lead-up to the Civil War. Both before and after that era, however, Christian scholars noted that the practice of race-based slavery was explicitly unbiblical. Racism (Galatians 3:28, Revelations 7:9), man-stealing (Exodus 21:16), and abusive servitude (Exodus 21:20) are all forbidden in the Bible.[21]

The first point of rebuttal against the idea that Genesis 9 teaches that black people are under a curse has already been mentioned: nowhere is race or skin color mentioned in that chapter. **Second**, Noah's curse is specifically imposed against Canaan, not Ham; so, in literal terms, there is no such thing as a "curse of Ham" in the Bible. Canaan, not Ham, was predicted to become a slave to his brothers, and had nothing to do with Africans – meaning Negroes. In fact, he settled in Asia Minor (not Africa). And even the meaning of Canaan's name had nothing to do with skin color, it meant "*down low*", "*that humbles and subdues*" in Hebrew.

The fulfillment of Noah's curse on Canaan occurred centuries later when the Israelites (who are from the line of Shem) entered the land of Canaan and subdued the inhabitants of that land (1 Kings 9:20-21) which eventually became Israel.

To conclude, the ideas of a "white race" and a "black race" were invented over the last five centuries influenced by European colonialism, in order to justify the enslavement of people of African descent by people of western European stock.[(22)]

At first when Caucasians left Europe, and went to other countries; they believed that they were superior to the other people whom they encountered in those lands; because of their Christian belief and their intellectual, philosophical, scientific achievements. They firmly believed in their racial superiority, in view of their belief that their god (small "g") in Christianity and his son (small "s") were also Caucasians – how wrong! It created the beginnings of the white supremacist erroneous way of thinking and the invented Aryan race[(23)] - actually, the word Aryan is a term used as an ethnocultural designation by Indo-Iranians in ancient times, and finds its roots in Central Asia not in Europe (see Encyclopedia Britannica for detailed explanation or Wikipedia article entitled "Aryan").

C. Aspects of Africa Leading to the Colonial Era Created by European Countries

This section shall cover three specific aspects of the subjugation of the Negro Ethnic Group (the Sub-Sahara African) to demonstrate their unfortunate impact on the persona and character of the Negro, and why they eventually helped create ideologies and movements, such as "La Négritude" so as to correct tremendous wrongs imposed on them. These three specific aspects are: Race, Slavery, and Colonialism. Each of these aspects dominated the Sub-Saharan scene for centuries, and inflicted irreparable damage on a people who are of a common ancestry and who in time created a tribal system of governance for each of their particular groups and sub-groups.

1. Race, A Biologically Misguided Designation

To recall, parts of Chapters II, III, and even this Chapter IV, has examined the lineage of the Negro, explained the concept of skin color as the basis of recognizing one ethnic group from another, looked into the creation of the word Negro, and how the issue of Biblical sin and curse was deceitfully taken advantage of by certain Europeans in order to determine that the Negro (the Sub-Sahara African) was inferior to them.

In this section, the definition of "race" is taken a step further, in that certain Europeans used the word "race" to make a convincing case about the Negro being inferior from a biological belief system instead of a Biblical point of view (i.e. sin of Ham and curse of Canaan). That meant that this new definition or designation for the word race was far more damning than the previous one (the Biblical as covered in the previous Section B).

The title "Race, A Biologically Misguided Designation" aims to suggest that the idea of race is not only misguided but also rooted in biological misconceptions. The title, therefore, is intentionally created in order to be thought-provoking as it invites readers to critically examine the biological basis of racial categorization.

In the extensive pathway or lane of human existence, the concept of race has been etched into societies, often shaping destinies, and defining futures. Yet, beneath the surface of this seemingly natural classification lies a profound misconception: race, as a biological construct, is an illusion, a misguided designation, which has been discredited by geneticists and anthropologists alike, who assert that genetic variation within human populations does not support the division of humanity into distinct racial categories.(24)

The Concept of Race

The term "race," which was occasionally used before the 1500s C.E., was applied to identify groups of people with a kinship or group connection. Historically, it was used in the sense of "nation" and "ethnic group". But after the 16th century C.E. the designation of the term race started to change so that by the 1800s C.E. it acquired its meaning in the field of physical anthropology through scientific racism (also termed biological racism).(25)

Scientific racism, sometimes termed **biological racism**, is the belief that mankind (or using the secular scientific term "human species") can be subdivided into biologically distinct races, and that provable and supportive evidence exists to justify racism be it racial discrimination, racial superiority, or racial inferiority.(26) Before the mid-20th century, scientific racism was accepted throughout the scientific community, and specifically among European and American academia.(27)

Since the second half of the 20th century, scientific racism has been discredited and criticized as obsolete. Along the same line, it was also said that the modern-day use of the term "race" is a human invention. In 2019, the American Association of Biological Anthropologists (formerly the AAPA) stated: "*The belief in 'races' as natural aspects of human biology, and the structures of inequality (racism) that emerge from such beliefs, are among the most damaging elements in the human experience both today and in the past.*" Nevertheless, it continues to be used, almost persistently, to support or validate racist worldviews based upon the belief in the existence and significance of racial categories and a hierarchy of superior and inferior races.(28)

Let us now observe or note what this misconstrued biologically misguided designation has caused in human suffering.

The Impact the Misguided Designation of Race Has Had on Whites and Blacks

During the European Enlightenment in the 17th and 18th centuries, philosophers and naturalists categorized the world anew, extending their thinking to mankind, to people. This resulted in redefining the term "race" into a human invention by identifying groups of people by physical traits, appearances, or characteristics – in other words classifying or categorizing race.

The concept of dividing mankind or humankind into three races called Caucasoid, Mongoloid, and Negroid was introduced in the 1780s by members of the Göttingen School of History (Germany) and further developed by Western scholars in the context of racist ideologies during the age of colonialism. This group of historians at this school played an important role in creating a scientific basis for historical research,(29) and were also responsible for created two fundamental groups of terminologies in scientific racism(30):

a. Blumenbach and Meiners's color terminology for race: Caucasian or white race, Mongolian or yellow race, Malayan or brown race, Ethiopian or black race, and American or red race;
b. Gatterer, Schlözer and Eichhorn's Biblical terminology for race; Semitic, Hamitic, and Japhetic.

(**Note:** Blumenbach is often called the "father of anthropology" or the "father of human racial science".)

By categorizing humans by "race," a new hierarchy was invented based on what many deemed to be science. From such categorization the false notion of "white" people being inherently smarter, more capable, and more human than "nonwhite" people was conceived and eventually became accepted worldwide. It is this type of categorization of people that became a justification for European colonization and subsequent enslavement of people from Africa.(31)

2. Slavery Stemming From Sub-Sahara Africa and The Slave Route

The enslavement of human beings occupies a painful and tragic space in world history. Denying a person freedom, autonomy, and life represents the worst kind of abuse of human rights.

One of the first written mentions (in cuneiform) of slavery was in the Mesopotamian Code of Hammurabi (c. 1860 BCE). However, it is a known fact that slavery existed much before the written word was invented.

Many societies tolerated and condoned human slavery for centuries. But in the 15th century C.E. an expanded and terrifying new era of enslavement emerged that has had a profound and devastating impact on human history.

Africans captured for the slave trade taken to market 18th Century C.E.

Slave caravan in East Africa 19th century C.E.
Credit: clu. Getty Images no. 1255573134.

British colonist trading with slaves in West Africa 1877 Original edition from my own archive Source: Tour du monde 1877 Drawing: Emile Bayard. Getty Images no. 1309077805.

Old engraved illustration of a convoy of female slaves, with children, in Angola, Central Africa, chained together and carrying heavy bundles. Credit: mikromano. Getty Images no. 1129685267.

After discovering lands that had been occupied by Indigenous people for centuries, European powers sent ships and armed militia to exploit these new lands for wealth and profit starting in the 1400s. In Sub-Sahara Africa, gold, sugar, tobacco, and extraordinary natural resources were viewed as opportunities to gain power and influence for Portugal, Spain, Great Britain, France, Italy, Germany, and Scandinavian nations.

Europeans first sought to enslave the Indigenous people who occupied these lands to create wealth for themselves. These foreign powers found cheap labor and so exploited to the maximum. It resulted in a catastrophic genocide as disease, famine, and conflict killed millions of Native people within a relatively short period of time.

Determined to extract wealth from these distant lands, as

European powers sought cheap labor from Africa, they launched a tragic era of kidnapping, abduction, and trafficking that resulted in the enslavement of millions of African people. They justified slavery of the Negro on the basis of their "new" designation of "race" which meant that the "inferior" African of black color could be enslaved by people of western European stock.

The enslavement of people has been a part of human history for centuries. Slavery and human bondage has taken many forms, including enslaving people as prisoners of war or due to their beliefs; but the permanent, hereditary enslavement based on race later adopted in Europe and the U.S. was rare prior to the 15th century.[(32)]

Many attributes of slavery began to change when European settlers, intent on colonizing the Americas, used violence and military power to compel permanent forced labor on enslaved people. Indigenous people became the first victims of forced labor and enslavement at the hands of Europeans in the Americas. As a result, in the decades that followed, millions of Indigenous people died from disease, famine, war, and harsh labor conditions.[(33)]

The Portuguese were the first to enter the Atlantic slave trade in the 16th century. For the next 4 centuries, they would remain the primary actors. In fact, by the time it was abolished in the 19th century, nearly half of all slaves traded in the Atlantic slave trade had been shipped to Portuguese colonies like Brazil.

Although most people think of the slave trade as being British ships taking slaves from West Africa to the United States, this only accounted for a little over 6% of all slaves. The vast majority of slaves (roughly 60%) were sent to Spanish and Portuguese South America. Most of the remaining slaves (about 30%) were taken to the Caribbean by the British, French, and Dutch Empires, and the balance to other geographical locations.(34)

The Main Slave Routes

Africans experienced three distinct types of slave trades: (a) The European Slave Trade that took Africans across the Atlantic from the mid-fifteenth century until the end of the 19th century C.E., (b) the Arab Slave Trade across the Sahara and the Indian Ocean that predated European contact with Africa, and (c) domestic slavery.(35) This meant that the slave trade involved complex networks of routes that spanned Europe, Africa, the Middle East, the Indian Continent, and the Americas.

Here are examples of the main slave routes:

The **Trans-Saharan slave trade**, part of the **Arab slave trade**, involved the transportation of slaves mainly across the Sahara Desert. Most were moved from Sub-Sahara Africa to North Africa to be sold to Mediterranean and Middle Eastern countries. Estimates of the total numberof black slaves moved from Sub-Sahara Africa to the Arab World range from 6 to 10 million, with the Trans-Sahara trade routes transported a significant number of this total (one estimate being around 7.2 million slaves crossing the Sahara from the mid-7th century C.E. until the 20th century C.E. at which time it was abolished. The Arabs managed and operated the Trans-Saharan slave trade, although Berbers were also actively involved.(35)

The **Red Sea slave trade**, sometimes known as the **Islamic slave trade**, Arab Slave Trade, or the **Oriental slave trade**, was a slave trade across the Red Sea trafficking Africans from the African continent to slavery in the Arabian Peninsula and the Middle East from antiquity until the mid-20th-century. When other slave trade routes were stopped, the Red Sea slave trade became internationally known as a "slave trade center" during the two World Wars. After World War II, growing international pressure eventually resulted in its final official stop.

The Red Sea Slave Trade was, together with the Trans-Saharan Slave Trade and the Indian Ocean Slave Trade, one of the arenas comprising what has been called the "Islamic Slave Trade" of enslaved people from East Africa to the Muslim World.[36]

The **Indian Ocean slave trade**, sometimes known as the **East African slave trade** and part of the Arab Slave Trade, was multi-directional slave trade and has changed over time. Captured in raids primarily south of the Sahara, predominately black Africans were traded as slaves to the Middle East, Indian Ocean Islands (including Madagascar),Indian Sub-Continent, and Java. Beginning in the 16th century, they were traded to the Americas, including Caribbean colonies.[37]

The **Atlantic slave trade** or **transatlantic slave trade** involved the transportation by slave traders of enslaved African people, mainly to the Americas. The outfitted European slave ships of the slave trade regularly used the Triangular Trade Route and its Middle Passage to the West Indies, and existed from the 16th to the 19th centuries.[38] The vast majority of those who were transported in the transatlantic slave trade were from Central and West Africa who had been sold by West African slave traders to European slave traders, while others had been captured directly by the slave traders in coastal raids; European slave traders gathered and imprisoned the enslaved at forts on the African coast and then brought them to the Americas.[39]

The colonial South Atlantic and Caribbean economies were

particularly dependent on slave labor for the production of sugar cane and other commodities such as coffee and cotton. This was viewed as crucial by those Western European states which were vying with one another to create overseas empires.(40) The Portuguese, in the 16th century, were the first to transport slaves across the Atlantic. In 1526, they completed the first transatlantic slave voyage to Brazil, and other Europeans soon followed. Shipowners regarded the slaves as cargo to be transported to the Americas as quickly and cheaply as possible, there to be sold to work on coffee, tobacco, cocoa, sugar, and cotton plantations, gold and silver mines, rice fields, the construction industry, cutting timber for ships, as skilled labor and as domestic servants.(41)

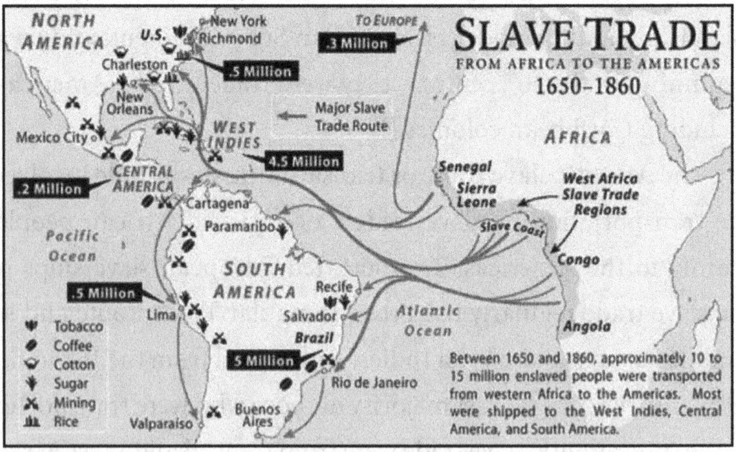

Map of the Slave Trade from Africa to the Americas

Historians estimate that approximately 12 million African slaves entered the Atlantic trade between the 16th and 19th centuries. About 1.5 million died on the ships during transport, and 10.5 million were sold into slavery, mostly in the Caribbean. Another 6 million were sold to Asian slave traders, and yet another 8 million were destined for slave markets on the continent of Africa itself.[42]

The **Barbary Slave Trade** involved slave markets in the Barbary States of North Africa – the name given to the coastal regions of central and western North Africa consisting of Algiers, Tunis, and Tripoli as well as the Sultanate of Morocco from the 16th to the 19th centuries C.E.[43]

European slaves were acquired by Muslim Barbary Pirates in slave raids on ships and by raids on coastal towns from Italy to the Netherlands, Ireland, and southwest of Britain as far north as Iceland and into the Eastern Mediterranean. The Mediterranean was the scene of intense piracy. As late as the 18th century, piracy continued to be a "consistent threat to maritime traffic in the Aegean Sea" – an elongated estuary of the Mediterranean Sea between Europe and Asia.[44]

This Photo of a Slave Ship Helped Energize The Movement Against Slavery 1788

Slaves In The Cellar Of A Slave Boat: Slaves in the cellar of a slave boat, c. 1830. Found in the Collection of Instituto Itau Cultural. Photo by Fine Art Images/ Heritage Images/Getty Images, no. 157479463.

Slave Ship: Lower Deck Stowage of Slaves - 18th Century C.E.

It is estimated that Slave Traders from Tunis, Algiers, and Tripoli enslaved 1 million to 1.25 million Europeans in North Africa, from the beginning of the 16th century C.E. to the middle of the 18th century C.E.(45)

The Barbary Pirates' interference in international trade between the USA and Europe prompted President Jefferson (in office 1801-1809) to wage war against the Barbary States. This war, which the U.S.A. won, took place from 1801 to 1804 and is considered to be the USA's first war against terror.

The Consequence of Enslavement on Sub-Sahara Africa

Continent in Millions:

	Year =	1650	1750	1850	1950
Africa		**100**	**95**	**95**	**200**
Europe		**100**	**140**	**265**	**530**

The adverse impact of slavery on Africa (and especially the Negro population) was enormous. During the 200-year period from 1650 to 1850, there was an increase in the European population of 165 million, whereas the population of Africa declined. One might say, quite correctly, that the Africans were being transported to the "New World." However, so were Europeans. Consequently, a substantial number of people were obviously missing primarily as a result of slavery.(46)

3. Colonialism, The Scramble for Africa

The **Scramble for Africa** (also more accurately called the "*Partition of Africa*" or the "*Conquest of Africa*") refers to the period between 1881 and 1914 when European powers significantly increased their influence in Africa. During this time, they invaded, divided, and colonized the continent. France and Britain played major roles in this process, with European control rising from around 10% to nearly 90% of Africa. Only two countries were free of colonial rule as of 1914: Ethiopia and Liberia.[47]

In 1884 the leaders of fourteen European countries and the United States came together to discuss control of Africa's resources. Known as **The Berlin Conference**, they sought to discuss the partitioning of Africa, establishing rules to "amicably" divide resources among the Western countries at the expense of the African people. Of these fourteen nations at the Conference, France, Germany, Great Britain, and Portugal were the major players – but what was noticeably evident at the conference is that representatives of Africa were not present, they were missing.[48]

The countries represented at the Conference were: Austria-Hungary, Belgium, Denmark, France, Germany, Great Britain, Italy, the Netherlands, Portugal, Russia, Spain, Sweden-Norway (unified from 1814 to 1905), Turkey, and the U.S.A.

The Berlin Conference 1884–1885 to legitimize the partition of Africa

The motivations behind the Scramble for Africa were primarily economic, political, and social. European powers sought to exploit Africa's resources, establish colonies, gain prestige, and secure strategic advantages. Their key exploitation objectives were as follows: **(a)** Economic interests that included access to raw materials, markets, and cheap labor; **(b)** Political interests, using colonial expansion as a way to demonstrate power and compete with other nations; and **(c)** Social interests, because of the belief in European racial superiority and a desire to "civilize" African societies (in other words to subjugate them). The Berlin Conference of 1884–1885 formalized the division of Africa among European powers.[(49)]

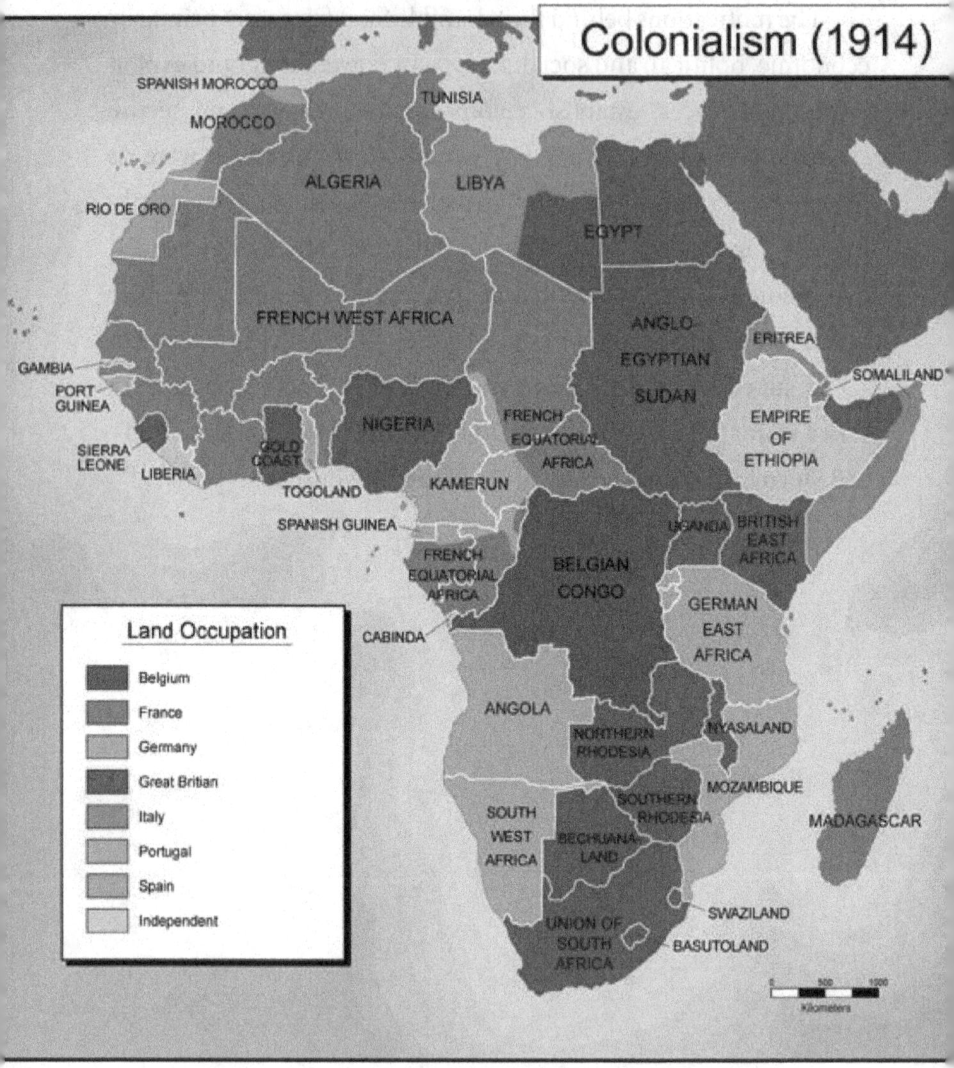

Historians have credited the scramble for Africa or the partition of Africa to "The Berlin Conference of 1884-1885".

In summary, it all resulted in the following:

- The Berlin Conference regulated and coordinated the partitioning of Africa among fourteen European countries and the United States
- The Scramble for Africa, of the period 1885 and 1914, allowed European countries to compete with each other for control of Africa's territories.
- Colonization of Africa meant the appropriating and settling of a territory, that when required, included the control by force over the indigenous people of that area.
- Imperialism meant the extension of authority and power by a nation over foreign countries through the acquisition of territories.

The Berlin Conference of 1884-1885. Dividing the African Pie Among the Colonizers.

Footnote:

1. History of Sub-Saharan Africa. (2022). *Essential Humanities.* Retrieved from http://www.essential-humanities.net/world-history/sub-saharan-africa/
2. "Africa", Encyclopedia Britannica. Africa: History, People, Countries, Map & Facts. Website: https://www.britannica.com/place/Africa by Alfred Kröner (Contributor)
3. *Mbiti, John S (1992). Introduction to African Religion.* When Africans are converted to other religions, they often mix their traditional religion with the one to which they are converted. In this way they believe that they are not losing something valuable, but are gaining something from both religious customs
4. Merriam-Webster Dictionary.com/dictionary/civilization/ and History of Sub-Saharan Africa. (2022). *Essential Humanities.*
5. "*Historical Survey: Slave Owning Societies*". Encyclopedia Britannica, 2007.
6. "*Demography, Geography, and the Sources of Roman Slaves*", by W.V. Harris, published in the *Journal of Roman Studies*, 1999.
7. "*Definition of Slave*", The Free Dictionary by Farlex.
8. "Saqaliba - *Slavs in the Arab World, Part 3* (*Slavs in Muslim Spain, part* (1)", "article by Niklot and Marek Kalisiński, July 2, 2017.
9. "*Where did the Word Slave Come From?*", Academic General Knowledge, 2023, Website: https://lisbdnet.com/where-did-the-word-slave-come-from/.
10. "*Origin Of The Word Slave*", The American Heritage® Dictionary of the English Language, Fourth Edition, Posted By: Siebra Muhammad, October 31st, 2011
11. "*Slavs of Muslim Spain*", by Michal Warczakowsk, The Apricity: A European Cultural Community, Website: www.theapricity.com, January 1, 2004.
12. "*The Meaning of Ethnicity: What It Is and How To Use It*", by Kevin Miller, The Word Encounter, June 30, 2022.

13. *"Late Latin"*, from The American Heritage Dictionary of the English Language (3rd edition), Boston, New York, London: Houghton Mifflin Company
14. *"How Do Race And Ethnicity Affect Identity?"* By Antonia Cirjak, in Society World Atlas, June 2, 2020.
15. Book Title: "Bible History of the Negro", by Richard Alburtus Morrisey, Originally Published 1915, Publisher: Independently published (May 7, 2020), Kindle Edition Location Pages 139-162
16. "*Why did Noah curse Canaan instead of Ham?*" by Got Questions Ministries, Colorado Springs, Colorado.
17. "*Why did Noah curse Canaan instead of Ham?*" by Got Questions Ministries, Colorado Springs, Colorado.
18. "*Why did Noah curse Canaan instead of Ham?*" by Got Questions Ministries, Colorado Springs, Colorado.
19. "*Are black people cursed?*" by Got Questions Ministries, Colorado Springs, Colorado.
20. "*Are black people cursed?*" by Got Questions Ministries, Colorado Springs, Colorado.
21. "*Are black people cursed?*" by Got Questions Ministries, Colorado Springs, Colorado.
22. Barnshaw, John (2008). "Race" In Schaefer, Richard T. (ed.). *Encyclopedia of Race, Ethnicity, and Society, Volume 1.* SAGE Publications. pp. 1091–3
23. Barnshaw, John (2008). "Race" In Schaefer, Richard T. (ed.). *Encyclopedia of Race, Ethnicity, and Society, Volume 1.* SAGE Publications. pp. 1091–3
24. *Retrieved from Microsoft Copilot AI-powered assistant.* From the American Psychological Association (APA) Microsoft Copilot. (May 11, 2024).
25. Kennedy, Rebecca F. (2013). "Introduction". Race and Ethnicity in the Classical world: An Anthology of Primary Sources in Translation. Hackett Publishing Company; p. xiii.

26. *Human Races Are Not Like Dog Breeds: Refuting A Racist Analogy"* by Norton, Heather; Quillen, Ellen; Bigham, Abigail; Pearson, Laurel; Dunsworth, Holly (July 9, 2019).
27. "*How Scientific Taxonomy Constructed the Myth of Race*" by Kenyon-Flatt, Britanny (March 19, 2021).
28. "*A Statement on Race and Racism*" from the American Association of Biological Anthropologists (formerly AAPA), 27 March 2019.
29. Burns, Robert M. (2006). Historiography: Foundations. Taylor & Francis. "The Old Cultural History", pp. 94-95.
30. Demel, Walter (1 November 2012). Race and Racism in Modern East Asia: Western and Eastern Constructions, pp 68-69. *Volume 1 of Brill's Series on Modern East Asia in a Global Historical Perspective.* Publisher BRILL 2012.
31. "*Historical Foundations of Race*", David R. Roediger, National Museum of African American History and Culture. Smithsonian Institution.
32. David Brion Davis, *Inhuman Bondage: The Rise and Fall of Slavery in the New World* (Oxford University Press, 2006), 27, 32; Jack Goody, "Slavery in Time and Space," in Asian and African Systems of Slavery, ed. James L. Watson (Berkley and Los Angeles: University of California Press, 1980), 25-27, 32-35.
33. Russell Thornton, American Indian Holocaust and Survival: A Population History Since 1492 (University of Oklahoma Press, 1987), 42-54.
34. *The Atlantic Slave Trade*, Written by Thomas Lewis. Editor Gloria Lotha The Editors of Encyclopedia Britanica, Inc. Jun 28, 2016.
35. Iddrisu, Abdulai (6 January 2023). "*A Study in Evil: The Slave Trade in Africa*"
36. Miran, Jonathan (2022-04-20), "*Red Sea Slave Trade*". Oxford Research Encyclopedia of African History, November 2023.
37. "*Indian Ocean and Middle Eastern Slave Trades*", by George M. La Rue, December 2020, Oxford Bibliographies.
38. "The History of the Trans-Atlantic Slave Trade", National Museums Liverpool July 2002.

39. *Gates Jr., Henry Louis, April 22, 2010, "Opinion: How to End the Slavery Blame Game".*
40. "The Rise and Fall of King Sugar", National Archives of Trinidad and Tobago. January 2023.
41. Berlin, Ira (9 April 2012). "The Discovery of the Americas and the Transatlantic Slave Trade".
42. "*The Way I See It - "The Missing 100+ Million"* **by** Jack Crawford, The Laguna Mobilization 2/21 Writers' Group (USA African Writers)**,** June 6, 2006.
43. *"Barbary: Historical Region, Africa", by Michael Brett.* The Editors of Encyclopedia Britannica. December 14, 2021.
44. Ginio, Eyal. "*Piracy and Redemption in the Aegean Sea During the First Half of the Eighteenth Century*". Turcica 33 (2001): 135-147.
45. Davis, Robert C. (2003). "*Christian Slaves, Muslim Masters: White Slavery in the Mediterranean, the Barbary Coast and* Italy (1500-1800)", p. 23. Palgrave Macmillan.
46. *"The Way I See It - "The Missing 100+ Million"* **by** Jack Crawford, The Laguna Mobilization 2/21 Writers' Group (USA African Writers), June 6, 2006.
47. Brantlinger, Patrick (1985). "Victorians and Africans: The Genealogy of the Myth of the Dark Continent". Critical Inquiry. 12 (1): 166-203
48. "*The Berlin Conference of 1884-85*", New World Encyclopedia, dated 29th August 2008.
49. *"Scramble for Africa", Encyclopædia Britannica, Inc./Kenny Chmielewski 2024.*

Chapter V

Socio-Historical Conditions: The Roots of La Négritude

As mentioned in the Preface, the words La Négritude are obviously French words. In English, they mean "Blackness" or more specifically they describe one's ethnicity, that is the Negro ethnic group.

The words **La Négritude** were coined in the 1930s and reflect a movement that emerged among French-speaking African and Caribbean writers living in Paris, France. It was a response to French colonial rule and French assimilation policies. It established, therefore, a valid strategy for "*la resistance*" against French colonialists.

Its leading figure was Léopold Sédar Senghor (elected in 1960 as the first president of the Republic of Senegal shortly after the country's independence from French rule) who, along with Aimé Césaire from Martinique (who actually coined the words), and Léon Damas from French Guiana, began to critically examine Western values and to reassess African culture – the three being Negro or Black intellectuals and writers from French speaking Sub-Sahara Africa, Caribbean, and South America.

Early on in the Négritude movement, the confirmation of Negro or Black pride was ascertained by loud cries against assimilating into the colonizer's political institutions and culture (including language) – "assimilation" was, obviously, an important element of French colonial policy. The movement felt that although it was theoretically based on a belief in universal equality, assimilation still assumed the superiority of European culture and civilization over that of the Negroid or Black African. They were also perturbed or unsettled by the two world wars because they saw their countrymen not only dying for a cause that was not theirs but also because they were being treated as inferiors on the battlefield.

The members of the Négritude movement became increasingly aware, through their study of history, of the suffering and humiliation of Black people first under the bondage of slavery and then under colonial rule. These views inspired many of the basic ideas behind Négritude:

- that the warm character of African life, regaining its closeness to nature and its constant contact with ancestors, should be continually placed in proper perspective against the materialism of Western culture;
- that Africans must look to their own cultural heritage to determine the values and traditions that are most useful in the modern world;
- that committed intellectuals and writers should use African themes or topics and poetic traditions in order to stimulate, or even provoke, a desire for political freedom;
- that Négritude itself should encompass the whole of African cultural, economic, social, and political values; and,
- that, above all, the value and dignity of African traditions and peoples must be asserted.

To be able to appraise the thinking behind the movement of La Négritude it is important to go to its roots so as to see how it came about and what exactly it reflects. Consequently, to understand La Négritude one must go back into the past to discern the social, economic, and political elements that have directed its movement and its way of thinking.

In this context, therefore, this chapter shall examine the socio-historical conditions that were able to effectively succeed in guiding the development of La Négritude. Therefore, first shall be constructed the characteristics of traditional Negro-African society as they existed prior to colonial contact; then an account of how colonialism affected that society shall be given; and finally, the chapter shall deal with the effect of the colonial presence on the present style of thought.

A. The "Communitary" Traditional Society: Tribalism, The Brotherhood

In the Negro-African society the family, which is the social unit, just like in any other society, is the center of that society. From that unit the various evolutionary stages of society are created and produced in concentric circles that become larger and larger: the family, the clan, the tribe, the nation, the country, the kingdom, the empire. Hence, the importance of the family in the Negro-African society since it lives and realizes itself in and through the society.(1)

A family unit is the extended family, the true family, composed of the descendants of the maternal ascendency in general because, as the Negro-African believed, the blood ties through the mother are definitely known. As it is said in Negro-African society "*it is the belly that ennobles.*"[2]

In principle, all the members of the extended family lived in the same area formed of many households and based on religious and economic foundations. At the head was the Chief of the Family who was the eldest man of the eldest generation. He was assisted by a family council of all the members who were of age. The council had the power to depose the Chief.[3]

The family chief was primarily in charge of the direction and supervision of the familial Community - that is, all its members. Secondly, he managed the familial wealth or property.

This represented inalienability (not transferable to someone else) and indivision (not divisible) of the community property because it belonged to all the members of the community. Not a single parcel was ceded definitely. Also, in all of life's circumstances, the Chief assisted the members of the community materially and morally.[4]

The family chief, like the village chief, was the one (as his position indicates) who exercised authority. He was the judge but he acted in accordance with the Family Council or Council of Elders.[5]

The Negro-African could not think of himself or herself apart from the community in which they lived. He or she were individuals belonging to an extended family. Thus, they saw themselves as members of a community in which they saw no struggles between an individual's own interests and those of the community, for the community was a definite extension of the family.

An individual might have had a conflict with another individual member of the same community, but with the community as a whole hardly any struggle existed. Hence, the Negro-African has been "communitary" in thinking and in the way of living; each individual was not a member of some artificial unit of human beings, but rather a member of a genuine community or what some would call a brotherhood or a kinship.[(6)]

Note: "communitary" means a member of a cooperative or a collectivist community. In today's terms, an example of such communitary entity would be a kibbutz or a type of settlement and collective community traditionally agrarian but now diversified into smallish manufacturing units and other businesses.

View of a 19th century C.E. Thatched Village House, Darfur (Western Sudan)

Traditional Village Thatched Huts of the Karamojong Tribes in Uganda

An Oasis Desert Village in Sub-Sahara Africa

Illustration of an African Village scene. Credit: Nastasic. Getty Images no. 1297621977

Illustration of an African Village scene. Credit: Nastasic. Getty Images no. 1297622124.

Antique illustration of African village. Credit: ilbusca. Getty Images no. 475715325

By separating or distancing "art and thought" from manual work, the Negro-African believed that contemporary society tended to emphasize material values to the detriment of spiritual values. It was presumed that the modern system of laws and rules governing private property alienated man in two conflicting ways: on the one hand, by depriving the individual from the products of his own work and effort; and, on the other hand, by perverting work itself.(7)

In Black Africa, that is traditional Negro-Africa, there almost never was property in the European sense of the word. A sense which refers to something that may be used or abused, that can be sold or destroyed. More precisely, the general means of production (that is, the soil and its wealth) could not be the objects of property in the European sense since first of all Negro-African animism makes of the soil a person, a spirit. The ancestral society, it is said, had concluded a pact with this spirit which was sanctioned by a ritual sacrifice. This pact, had not been concluded in the name of an ancestor or ancestors, but in the name of the collectivity and for the collectivity that the ancestor(s) represented in the name of future generations.[(8)]

Hence, from where came the idea that there is no right of property in the Negro-African traditional society, not even possessive rights. Rather it is a right of usufruct (i.e., the right of using and enjoying the fruits or profits of something belonging to the collectivity), and here the chief has had a role to supervise the integrity and the good usage of the collectivity of the land. He is the one who reserved certain portions for collective exploitation and distributed the land between the households by instituting a rotation system in order that the same households did not always have the good or the bad land. Work or man's productive action was considered as the sole source of property and he could confer the right of property only on what he had produced.[(9)]

From the above account of the use of property and the individual's work, one can see that the general means of production was a collective issue, production being the object of collective property. In such a society, man was assured at least the minimum needs of food, shelter, and clothing.

In such a society (a communitary entity), the belief was that man is tied to the object of property where property, as the means of production, is no longer something abstract. Man felt he is not a simple component of his soil or of his toil. Rather, he felt and he knew that his intelligence and his arms created something that is alive (a living thing) and that his work itself was not a duty but a source of joy. In this respect, it permitted a harmony between man and his community.[10]

In conclusion, the main features of the traditional Negro-African society can be summed up as follows: **first**, the authority of the people (especially the old) was represented in the Chief and the Council of Elders or the Family Council; **second**, solidarity was imprinted on the very basic structure of Negro-African society, and especially in its economic organization; **finally**, there was an egalitarian character and spirit in the Negro-African society. This is seen, for instance, in the fact that property was common, there was no class that accumulated the capital property and reduced others to the state of mere tenancy, and exploitation of man by man never became part of the system. As for the political aspect, the Chief was not an absolute ruler since he was restricted by a council which could annul or oppose acts of the chief if it was deemed not in the interest of the collective.

B. Colonialism

Colonialism did not exactly come with the slave trade, rather it came after. However, the Western European Countries believed that their first contact of Black Africa through the slave trade gave them an opportunity to enhance their world positions and interests by way of colonizing that part of the globe.

Therefore, the idea of an era of colonialism started with Europe's first contact with Black Africa; hence, its importance in this section and chapter. Another important factor is that the slave trade was a common denominator in developing color pride and race consciousness among Blacks, the Negro-African.

Probably no single experience has so deeply influenced the Sub-Sahara Africans as their years of domination by Western colonial powers - primarily United Kingdom of Great Britain, France, Germany and to a lesser degree Italy, Portugal, Spain, Belgium, Holland.

In most of the African continent the political orientation and structure, the economic organization and disabilities that followed, and the disintegration of the traditional social structure may be strongly traced to the practice and impact of the colonial powers. It might also be important to mention that the Muslim Arab Traders who settled in many parts of the continent starting in the eighth century C.E. had an important role in disabling and fragmenting the traditional tribal structure prevailing in Sub-Sahara Africa be it by being directly involved in the slave trade even before the involvement of the Europeans or the exploitation of the natural resources at the expense of the locals.

European Man Stands Astride Over The Whole Of Africa. Portraying Cecil Rhodes.

1. The Immediate outcome of the European Contact With Africa: The Slave Trade and Its Impact on Race Consciousness and Color Pride

The European navigators of the 15th century came to the West coast of Africa. Europe wanted to dominate nature and develop her industry. The difficult conditions that Sub-Sahara Africa nature presented were to activate Europeans to push towards regions that would enhance economic development.(11)

At the beginning, Europeans needed outposts or coastal stations to help the ships on their long sea voyage to India and the East Indies round the Cape. As time passed, Europeans started to trade with the natives for such goods as gold, ivory, gum, and then for slaves. The Europeans exchanged their goods for slaves for they saw they could make great profits by selling them to the New World where manpower was very much needed.[(12)]

This first European contact with African society had at best negative and disruptive effects because slave trade extracted millions of men, women and children, who in most societies are responsible for a major portion of the physical and creative effort. The disruptive effect which slaving had was that the white man had the opportunity to point to what he often chose to call the "innate inferiority" and "moral degeneracy" of the Negro, even accusing them from a religious point of view. Gradually, the slave trade became progressively destructive to any possible "culture evolution" or growth. It provoked wars, gave economic sanctions to human brutality, and oppressed any normal cultural and economic development in Africa and starting in West Africa and then finding its way to the rest of Sub-Saharan Continent.[(13)]

The nineteenth century marked the decline of European slave trading. But its effects remained. Moreover, to consolidate the situation of "white versus black" was the colonization, conquest, and missionary activity which accompanied, or almost immediately followed, the slave trade.[(14)]

Race consciousness and color pride were to be the primary outcome of the slave trade which culminated in the need of liberating the African personality from the European imposition of the Master-Slave or Master-Subject status.[(15)]

2. The Transformation of the Traditional Society: A Loss of Identity or Depersonalization

As political and economic development in Europe shifted from the stage of unification to that of industrialization, the European powers sought in the colonies a further way of increasing their wealth and development, and accordingly their status and prestige in world affairs.

The policies and the positions of the colonialists in the subject territories were means to satisfy ends. This was reflected in the exploitation of the colonies for the aggrandizement of the metropolitan countries guided primarily by economic, political, and military considerations and hidden, as many eminent personalities on the subject believe, behind the idea of the "White Man's Burden" which the colonialists tried to institutionalize as a legend.[16a]

Note: "*White Man's Burden*" is defined by the Merriam-Webster Dictionary as a duty formerly asserted by white people to manage the affairs of non-white people whom they believe to be inferior to them. Rudyard Kipling (1865-1936), who was a white supremacist, authored a book in 1899 entitled "*The White Man's Burden*" in which he describes this concept as well as the justification for colonialism and imperialism by the Europeans.

Now, all the things that men and groups did in Negro-Africa, were done in the context of the colonial situation. This colonial situation and the power behind it was able to produce changes.

The first change brought about by colonialism was the creation of the national symbol of the state. Most of the states in Africa did not exist as national entities before their colonization by the European powers. The idea of "nation" was foreign to most African societies – the exceptions were the countries of North Africa.[16b]

With foreign penetration in the area, nation states were created. Their size, shape, and nature were determined by the extent of local resistance and by competition from other colonial powers. Thus, boundaries of the colonial territories were determined by imperial ambitions rather than ethnic, linguistic, or political consideration. It was a formalistic political framework held together more by force and superior technology than by the sentiment on the part of individuals that they were members of a common national community.[16c]

Because tribal, ethnic, and linguistic groups were divided by colonial boundaries, and because the minorities were not sufficiently socialized into the colony, the individual group's loyalty often remained with a regional group which cut across the new boundaries. The borders drawn up in the nineteenth and twentieth centuries were responsible for a lack of national unity and loyalty in a number of countries – in fact the colonialists had imposed artificial boundaries on the Negro Tribal Groups. For example, in West African countries, the lines of the boundaries go inland from the coast, cutting across the traditional, ethnic, tribal, and religious bounds that are the same as along the coast.[17]

Though the boundaries imposed by the colonial rulers provoked a number of divisive forces they, nevertheless, provided for the creation and establishment of the national state systems. The boundaries established the framework within which nationalistic leaders had to function, and they were to be inherited by those very same nationalistic leaders upon independence from the colonial powers that occupied them (the territorialization and the delimitation of the boundaries of all the African political entities by the colonial administrations coincide with the present-day boundaries of most of the newly independent countries).[18a]

In spite of the fact that the symbol of the nation-state was a great innovation, people and especially leaders had a feeling that the colonial governments were instituting political regression and were adding tension to the "inferiority complex" that they had created.[18b]

The colonial powers, apart from carving the boundaries of Africa creating artificial nations or countries, introduced new **economic elements**:[19a]

- they changed the economy from a subsistence to a money economy;
- they introduced the cash crops and elements of economic individualism;
- they created a wage labor force to meet the labor demands of the European enterprises.

On the **social side**, the much improved and expanded means of communication and transportation resulted in migrations from the traditional units of loyalty to the cities or towns. We find rapid development of urban centers, and the imposition of a common language - the one of the ruling colonial power. The role of the traditional rulers or chiefs decreased because they were generally used as agents (this brought distrust and weakened the loyalties once found between the masses and the traditional rulers). Finally, there was the spread of modern education.[19b]

All this was not a gratuitous gift from Europe. A modern society, however limited in scope, needs human resources to run it, work it, and staff the offices. Therefore, it created the need for a trained workforce which the colonial governments could not do without if they wanted to run the colonies.

The transformation of the traditional Sub-Saharan society did bring positive elements, such as the infrastructure. It created a new elite whose emergency was the single most important consequence of the social change. But with these came along negative elements, such as the economic dependence on paternalistic capitalism which gave enormous profits to the big companies while the standard of living of the masses had not improved and was still miserable. Moreover, colonialism in all its stages revealed a "white supremacy" whether as direct racial superiority or as cultural superiority - corresponding to the destruction of the values of the traditional Negro-African civilizations, which consequently replaced such values by those imported by the colonialists.[(20)]

Hence, the African personality (its persona and character) was displaced from its original surroundings and was transplanted into a completely different one where the task of adaptation was very difficult and in which the Master-Subject relation and the denigration of Negro-Africa's past prevailed. This later caused for the search and the re-creation of the lost identity and the need for the revival of the authenticity of the Sub-Saharan African soul, more specifically the Negro soul.

3. The Notion of White Supremacy and the Process of Assimilation: The Birth of Anti-Colonialism and Anti-Imperialism

The notion of "White Supremacy" was introduced to Negro-Africa through the idea that because Europeans were superior in technology, they were superior in all things; and in the early phase many accepted this idea.[21] There were other more flagrant issues than technology that were imposed on the Negro societies as well, as covered in previous chapters.

The Negro-African was "educated" to believe that he was inferior and that the white man was superior, for the white educators often tended to denounce everything African as "savage, primitive, and pagan". The fact of conquest, whether by force of arms, missionary, signing treaties, or other, was also made proof of European superiority.[22]

Apart from the above notion of white supremacy, the white man had assigned himself the duties of trusteeship and a civilizing mission in respect of what he called the backward peoples or the Dark Continent.[23]

The alternative notion to that of white supremacy is, without doubt, complete rejection of the whole idea. Those who tended most strongly and earliest to doubt white supremacy were the "evolues" as the French called them, the assimilados by Portuguese standard, or the educated elite as the British named them. Whatever was European was considered best. And the Negro-African would be accepted (that is assimilated) when and if he "evolved" into a Frenchman for instance, which he could do by adopting and believing in everything French, or British, or Portuguese, as the case may be. As would be expected, such a new type of "education" of Negro-Africans created a class who very quickly became aware of the inadequacy of the idea of white superiority. Consequently, they started to oppose this notion as well as colonialism.[24]

Antagonized by the realities of colonial rule while educated in and aware of the ideals of the European national image, the new elites eventually asserted themselves with a nationalistic fervor that made real the possibility of national self-determination[25]. Moreover, as the native peoples substituted the values of their traditional society for those of a Euro-industrial one, there was an increasing realization that only modernization and industrialization could produce the better society at home (which the new elites had come to admire abroad, and so be able to satisfy the "rising expectations" of the people).[26]

The new elites now came to realize that colonialism was in opposition to industrialization, in part because the colonial powers did not want industries in the colonies that would compete with their own as they relied on colonial supply of cheap raw materials and quick access to colonial markets. This realization generally caused the new elites to believe that modernization constituted a threat to colonialism and, therefore, to colonial powers.[27]

The result of all the above was that the new elites **first** responded with cries of anti-colonialism and anti-imperialism, **then** with nationalism which encouraged the various movements to move towards independence, and **finally** the development of color pride and cultural pride. In addition, the new elites started to consider any criticism of Africa or Africans (regardless of whether they were in the North or whether they were located in Sub-Sahara) as a criticism against their personality, their character – the type of criticism that the new elites believed the colonialists were trying to depersonalize them from their original roots and therefore deemed unacceptable.

4. Nationalism and the Ouster of the Colonialists: A reaction to the Conditions that Imposed Domination

As previously mentioned, all the arguments about economic and political subservience, social scorn, and the like were imposed by white persons upon black persons. This provided the elements of dissatisfaction and discontent which emerged in the "active minority", as the new elite was called. These elements, moreover, provided for the cries of anti-colonialism which in turn brought about nationalism, or more exactly colonial nationalism, since it was colonial rule which unconsciously paved the way for the rise of such nationalism.

In a way, the development of Negro-African nationalism was considered to be a progressive and positive change of form or of character in what would be acceptable as an adequate expression of racial and cultural equality. Therefore, the Negro-African began to develop a nationalism that was an immediate reaction to colonialism and to the conditions that imposed inferiority.(28)

Now, the new elites believed that equality could be achieved through the freedom that independence could provide. Therefore, to win the fight for independence it was important to make the masses aware of their unequal positions, awaken a desire for freedom, and to arouse resentment of the colonialists. Once the allegiance of the masses was gained, the battle was won and the "*transfer of power and sovereignty*" was only a matter of time.[29]

C. Effects of the Past on the Present

The effect of colonial rule was that Sub-Sahara Africans in general did not want the colonial relationship anymore. This was and continues to be a basic desire: to see colonialism ended, and the vestiges of colonialism in any form removed. It is wrong to assume that this desire is confined as an attitude of hostility to the West. Rather, it is the desire to be free Black men, the desire of Negro-Africans to finally be independent – in fact, an instinct taught by the colonial powers. Such sentiment remains strong and everything that Black or Negro-Africans do to solve their own problems is embraced by this emotionalism.[30]

Joseph Ki-Zerbo, a Burkina Faso (formerly called Upper Volta) "evolue", said in his article "African Personality and the New African Society":

> *Colonialism had inflicted a gigantic trauma on the African personality. It was a tragic side-tracking of the African personality toward ideals and roles that have adulterated it. Thus, the African personality has become a sort of shipwreck towed along by the thread of a history made and written by the European conquerors, the final aim of the colonizers being to annex the mentality and concepts of the colonized people.*

Therefore, there came a need to identify with the Negro-African society as it prevailed before the era of colonialism:[31a]

- there came a need to reassert and revive the past through a search for identity which emphasized African pride in accomplishments;
- there came the need to assert the independence of African opinion and world view and in the insistence on a strict observance of sovereignty and equality within the world community; and finally,
- there came the desire to contribute to world civilization in a way which is universally recognized and acclaimed.

These impulses show themselves again and again in the efforts to develop a uniquely African personality, that would ensure that Negro-Africans would cherish their freedom to work out their destiny in their own way and not in ways imposed upon them by outsiders.[31b]

Devotion to the traditional Negro-African society spread everywhere, in a way that did not mean the refusal or rejection of modernization or industrialization, but rather as a way of preserving the soul and spirit rather than institutions. This has meant that Negro-Africans would praise and advance their "communitarian" traditional solidarity as well as their exposure and association with nature, implying a certain type of solid relation between humans and also between humans and their world.[32]

"Africanism", or as it happened, what has been called Négritude, developed with the mission of re-establishing the pride of Negro-Africans in themselves, and in propagating the "new truth" about Negroes and about Negro-African culture.[33]

Footnote:

1. Leopold Sedar Senghor, Liberte: Negritude et Humanisme (Paris: Le Seuil,1964), pp. 49-50.
2. Alioune Sene, Negritude et Revolution Africaine, une conference donnee par l'Ambassadeur du Senegal au Caire au Centre D'Etudes Dar es Salaam (le Caire: La Conference, Mardi 24 Janvier, 1972), pp. 4-5.
3. Fenner Brockway, African Socialism (Pennsylvania: Dufour Editions, 1963), pp. 25-29.
4. "Dakar Colloquium: Search for Definition," Africa Report, Vol. 8, No. 5 (May 1963), p. 18.
5. L.S. Senghor, Liberte: Negritude et Humanisme, p.270.
6. Dakar Colloquium, p.18.
7. Ibid.
8. L.S. Senghor, Liberte: Negritude et Humanisme, p. 273.
9. Ibid, p. 274.
10. Ibid., pp. 275-277.
11. C.C. Wrigley, "Historicism in Africa: Slavery and State Formation," African Affairs, Vol. 70 (April 1971), p. 114.
12. Robert A. July, The Origin of Modern African Thought (New York: Frederick A. Praeger, 1967), p. 459.
13. Austin J. Shelton, "The Black Mystique: Reactionary Extremes in Negritude", African Affairs, Vol. 69 (April 1964), p. 116.
14. C.C. Wrigley, African Affairs, p. 119.
15. Ibid, p. 120.
16. 16abc. Fred P. Von der Mehden, Politics of the Developing Nations (Englewood Cliffs, N.J.: Prentice Hall, Inc., 1964), pp. 37-38.
17. Ibid., p. 38.

18ab. "L'Afrique en Devenir: Essai sur L'Avenir de L'Afrique Noir," Perspective, XIII (June 1966), p.36.

19ab. I. Wallerstein, The Politics of Independence (New York: Alfred A. Knopff, Inc., 1961), pp. 31-43.

20. A. J. Shelton, African Affairs, p. 126.
21. Ibid, p. 116.
22. Ibid, p. 117
23. William J. Hanna, Independent Black Africa: The Politics of Freedom (Chicago: Rand McNally and Company, 1964), p. 161.
24. J. H. A. Watson, "French Speaking Africa Since Independence", African Affairs, Vol. 62 (July 1963).
25. Robert I. Rotberg, "African Nationalism", The Journal of Modern African Studies, Vol. 4 (May 1966), 39-40.
26. J. H. Kautsky, Political Change in Underdeveloped Countries: Nationalism and Communism (New York: John Wiley and Sons Inc., 1967), p. 47.
27. Ibid, p. 48.
28. W. J. Hanna, p. 14.
29. Ibid, p. 14-15.
30.

31ab. J. H. A. Watson, pp. 218-219.

32. Perspective, pp. 18-19.
33. Ibid, pp. 22, 29, 30.

Chapter VI

La Négritude: A Social Humanism

As previously mentioned, the **Négritude** movement emerged among French-speaking Black intellectuals in the 1930s. Initially, it was a literary, cultural, and poetic response to colonial oppressions.

Shaped by anti-colonial and Pan-Africanist ideas, Négritude envisioned a world founded in equality and justice. It rejected French colonial racism and celebrated Black identity, triggering an awakening of race consciousness across Black Africa and the Black African Diaspora.

Négritude was a response to colonial oppression. But, it was also more than just a political movement, with culture and art at the heart of its development and approach. In addition, the use of poetry and literature ensured that it was founded not only in the struggle against colonial presence and the desire for political change but also in creativity and artistry.(1)

The Négritude movement was a response, by Black Caribbean and African elites studying in Paris, to their strong awareness of injustice, both in the context of colonialism and in their own experience living in the European metropole.

Léopold Sédar Senghor, Aimé Césaire, and Léon-Gontran Damas where the three who were regarded as the founders of the movement - a movement which intended to answer the question of "*Who am I*?" in response to the dehumanizing practices of racism, colonialism, and the injustices associated with assimilation politics.

As a consequence, Négritude sought to explore, reclaim, and celebrate what Blackness was meant to be in a world that mostly looked at the Negro in a racialized, marginalized, and oppressed way. It resulted in developing a social humanism with its roots embedded in the Negro-African traditional persona, which meant the inclusion of language to reinforce ones identity and locality – in other words, the movement encouraged the use of indigenous African languages and promoted cultural pride as well.

This all meant that Négritude would not only be an expression of the desire to become "*mentally emancipated*" from the colonial presence (which imparted a feeling of inferiority, alienation, disequilibrium), but also a desire to create a sense of security that would allow the adoption of positive changes from outside the African character, the African persona. As a renowned African person had once said: "*We are willing to assimilate what you offer us, but not to be assimilated by you*".(2)

Note: This African person was Edward Wilmot Blyden (1832–1912), who was an Americo-Liberian educator, writer, diplomat, and politician primarily active in West Africa. The quote he referred to was made in a lecture he gave entitled "*Study and Race*," delivered in Sierra Leone, Freetown on May 19th, 1893. Blyden challenged racist scientific theories.

In summary, Négritude was a powerful response to colonialism, racism, and cultural removal of ancestral traditions and history. Its impact extended beyond literature as it shaped political thought, cultural movements, and the fight against colonialism .... as it celebrated Blackness, affirmed identity, and laid the groundwork for a more inclusive and just world.

This chapter shall describe the above mentioned aspects in some more detail; but, prior to doing so, a brief idea of what Negritude specifically is shall be explained.

A. What Is Négritude?

The concept of Négritude, as we have seen in previous chapters, basically consists of a response or a reaction on three levels:[3a]

- The first level is the slave trade which brought about the notion of African inferiority and white supremacy, and gave rise to race consciousness and color pride.
- The second level is colonialism which transformed the traditional Negro-African society into a modern society, disregarding tribal affiliations and creating artificial states, in which a loss of identity of the group was the outcome.
- The third level goes much beyond all others whereby Négritude consists of a positive movement striving toward unity of the group. It represents the Negro-African's attempt to find for his group a normal self-pride and a "world in which he again has a sense of identity and a significant role".

Therefore, Négritude is the totality of Negro-African values which expresses impulses, passions, and attitudes created as a result of socio-historical and political implications.[3b]

To take it even further, it can be said that Négritude is a matter of form, of some innate emotional quality of the Negro soul which binds Negroes in Africa and elsewhere. Hence, Négritude is "*the complex whole of Negroid civilized values – cultural, social, political, and economic – which describes the character of black peoples, or, more exactly the Negro-African*".(4)

Put in realistic but intricate or complex terms, Négritude is the combination of a people's mental and social adaptation or transformation, which would allow the worthy development of a positive and genuine "*global output*". The problem to overcome is, therefore, routine inferiority complexes, and the fatalistic spirit. In a word it is to awaken the consciousness to the call of Négritude.(5)

Just like any other nation, continent, or bloc that exists by means of models, Black Africa must as well (for what are free enterprise, democracy, or communism if not models around which millions shape their lives?). In effect, Négritude is a model, an ideology which has developed with its own circumstances into a form of social humanity.(6)

In the struggle for freedom, human dignity, and social reassertion, Négritude offers an ideological alternative to communism, western democracy, or other political systems. It ideally stands for racial coexistence on the basis of complete equality and freedom, and respect for human personality. It preferably looks above the limitations of class, race, tribe, religion (that is, it wants equality for all; and attempts to stretch beyond the limits of the nation-state's frontiers).(7)

Thus, Négritude is a "black light" meant to illuminate the true and proper value of the Negro-African coupled with an attempt to create a "new truth". In a nutshell, and generally stated, the main elements that form the character and personality of this movement resonate from the following:

- Reaction to colonialization: Denunciation of Europe's colonial lack of humanity, and rejection of Western domination.
- Identity crisis: Acceptance of and pride in being black; preserving and enhancing of African history, traditions, and beliefs.
- Reaction to disunity, artificial boundaries: the civilization of the universal; unity of the races, nations, and continents.
- Very realistic artistic and literary styles.

A Sub-Sahara African artistic expression of serenity and hope for a bright future.

As a result, the black light of La Négritude that radiated so significantly with so many prominent issues that helped the

Negro-African regain the character and persona of old ended influencing political movements in several ways:

1. **African Nationalism and Independence Movements:**
   - Négritude fostered a sense of African identity and pride, inspiring nationalist movements across the continent.
   - Leaders like Kwame Nkrumah (Ghana), Jomo Kenyatta (Kenya), and Julius Nyerere (Tanzania) drew upon Négritude ideals in their quests for independence from the colonialist.

2. **Anti-Colonial Resistance:**
   - Négritude challenged colonial narratives that portrayed Africans as inferior.
   - It encouraged resistance against oppressive colonial regimes, advocating for self-determination and sovereignty.

3. **Cultural Revival:**
   - Négritude celebrated African culture, languages, and traditions.
   - This cultural revival fueled movements to reclaim indigenous practices and reject Western cultural dominance.

4. **Pan-African Solidarity:**
   - Négritude emphasized unity among Black people globally.
   - It laid the groundwork for Pan-Africanism, promoting collaboration and shared goals.

B. La Négritude and Cultural Consciousness

Leopold S. Senghor once said that "culture is the first requisite and the final objective of all developments". The quote emphasizes the central role of culture in shaping human progress. Culture encompasses language, beliefs, customs, art, rituals, and more. It includes both **tangible aspects** (like historical facts and institutions) and **intangible aspects** (like traditions and values).[8a]

Culture is not only an accessory but a fundamental aspect of development. It highlights the importance of considering cultural dimensions when formulating policies and strategies for sustainable growth and well-being. Here are two examples that demonstrate the importance of culture, how it can affect the Negro-African persona and its role in developing the ideology of La Négritude:[8b]

- **Culture Shapes Identity**: Culture defines who we are as individuals and communities. It influences our values, traditions, and ways of life. Recognizing culture's role is essential for achieving inclusive and equitable development.
- **Human-Centered Development**: Placing culture at the heart of development policies ensures that progress benefits people directly. It promotes a comprehensive and complete approach that goes beyond economic growth to encompass well-being, social cohesion, and environmental sustainability.

In addition, the fact is that Negro-Africans need to be themselves in their dignity, in their regained identity – to be themselves means cultivating their own values as they rediscover them in the birthplace of the Negro-African environment. Consequently, culture-consciousness is the needed impetus or stimulus for Negro-Africans to be themselves, not without borrowing and not by procuration, but rather by their own personal and collective efforts. Otherwise, Negro-Africans will perceive that they will simply be poor copies.

From a different view, culture could also be defined as "*the civilization in action or the spirit of the civilizations*". In other words, it would be the result of a double effort of "*integration of Mankind to nature, and of nature to Mankind*". By nature is meant the physical environment, and Mankind (to live in it) would have to adapt to it. This has meant that the physical environment has allowed the gaining of information related to economic and social structures and also to art and philosophy. It all boils down to Mankind transforming nature in order to submit it to the exigencies of life.[9a]

Painting of a Sub-Sahara Africa Contemporary Village Scene.

Therefore, culture can be considered an action, a revolutionary action, an action by Mankind; and this is what distinguishes Mankind from animals. Here, revolutionary action is defined as a "real movement or momentum" that would suppress and replace the colonial administration, instituted in the name of progress, which to the Negro-African was in reality equivalent to political regression – as demonstrated in Chapter V. In the traditional Negro-African tribal system, political emancipation to the Negro-Africans meant that everybody participated in the election of the Elders, that the individual or the person was protected by the communitarian customs and family type of environment.[9b]

When culture is defined as an equilibrium between man and his/her social and natural environment, it demonstrates that this culture can be maintained only if the Negro-African conserves his/her personality, even if it means integrating cultural values that are other than his or hers. In this sense, therefore, the rehabilitation of the traditional culture is not exactly the preservation of the old values but rather the safeguarding of the personality – which means that the Negro-African personality only claims the protection of the still existing traditional values. This implies that culture should not be the result of adding and subtracting traditional Negro-African values from European values, but should imply a completeness that consists of its whole potential, its whole fabric.[10]

Also, the claim to a culture in the past does not only restore the Negro-African personality but serves as a justification for the hope of a future culture. In psycho-affective equilibrium the claim to a culture is responsible for an important change in the Negro-African because of the absolute condemnation by Colonialism of pre-colonial society and pre-colonial history, and the colonial belief that the "*darkest lights of humanity*" existed in that period.[11]

Painting of Women carrying baskets on their heads going to the market.

Adherence to Negro-African culture and to the cultural unity of Negro-Africa is arrived at by confirming without conditions the fight of the people for freedom. No one can sincerely wish for the spread of Negro-African culture if it does not give virtual support to the creation of the conditions needed for the existence of that culture; that is, in short, to the liberalism and freedom of the entire community.[12]

Painting of an African traditional tribal village remote from any city, from the eyes of a modern artist.

To conclude, although in traditional Negro-African society art and music took priority over productive labor and technical activities, contemporary Negro-African society cannot deny the industrial world. It needs industrialization for human progress. Yet, in the desire for rapid industrialization, the Negro-African must not sacrifice his spiritual, moral, and artistic values for the Western or European technical supremacy that is concerned only with the exterior of man. Only by an equilibrium between the material and moral values can Negro-African culture make a worthwhile contribution to humanity. In other words, the humanism of Négritude will help Negro-Africans deliver themselves from the anti-humanistic civilization of Europe now dominated by materialism and machines; and through the expression of Negritude, Negro-Africans will secure an independence from the European elements of dominance and disunity.(13)

Hence, all the efforts of Negro-Africans to rediscover their historical past tend to define and to affirm their culture-consciousness and the need to achieve a coherent "world image"; and, therefore, once again, reflect an important aspect of Négritude.

C. The Civilization of the Universal: The Unity of the Races

Bearing in mind what the Negro-African went through with the slave trade, race, colonialism, the creation of nation-states disregarding tribal affiliations, etc., the importance of unity becomes crucial.

Négritude has, as one of its ideological aims, the interdependence of ethnic groups, races, nations, and continents. This would mean a de-territorialized continent and world where all races and nations would find unity. With this in mind, common terms that arouse deep emotional reactions and express aspirations such as sovereignty, independence, autonomy, collective wills, the will of the state, can no longer be used interchangeably.(14)

Celebrating Diversity. Illustration of large group of people with distinctive characteristics. Credit: aelitta. Getty Images no. 1368244378.

Could such a world ever be achieved? It is very unlikely that the whole world would unite as one, though efforts have been made on a smaller scale to form regional zones such as the European Union. By the same token Africa has embraced Pan-African Solidarity and La Négritude has laid the groundwork for Pan-Africanism by promoting collaboration and shared goals among all African nations. As a result, Pan-African thought influenced the establishment of the Organization of African Unity (since succeeded by the African Union in 1963) with its headquarters in Addis Ababa, Ethiopia – which created a shared identity and sense of community but not united as one state.

Note: Pan in Pan-Africanism means "all", "of everything", or "involving all members of a group".

To express the spirit of liberty and unity, La Négritude believes that the Negro-African must have the freedom of choice between civilizations that are in contact. Moreover, though the aftereffects of colonialism remain, they must be absorbed or transcended so as to emerge from the alienation of the past. Therefore, there should be a stop in the denunciation and attribution of resentments and bitterness towards colonialism. Examined in perspective, colonization would then appear at first glance as a general fact of history.[15a]

The Pan- African Union Emblem: representing the continent of Africa (with the stars representing the countries in Africa).

Also, because the main objective is the progress of Mankind there must be an exchange of civilizations so that by "cross-fertilization" civilizations can have new life, new meaning, and new purpose. Here a dialectic process is employed from which progress results from the union of opposites. The thesis affirms, the antithesis negates, and the synthesis unites what is only valid in the thesis and antithesis. In other words, the thesis is the foreign civilization, the antithesis is La Négritude, and the synthesis is the "*Civilization of the Universal*" – in other words, the unity of the races, of the different civilizations, of the valid values in "foreign civilizations" and in "Négritude" with the exclusion of what is considered to be adverse to the growth and development of the new universe.[(15b)]

In short, both Negro-African and foreign civilizations have contributions to make in the establishment of the Civilization of the Universal. For instance, the Negro-African society could contribute its ethical-spiritual communitarian values and other societies could contribute the principal technical means that have helped them to develop (that is, one contributes its humanism and the other its material welfare). Therefore, the ideal is the creation of the Civilization of the Universal through which unity of the races becomes possible because the complementary differences would be fused and live on together in symbiosis and, in so doing, put an end to alienation in the world.(16) Interestingly, all great civilizations have been mixtures of disparate elements. Hence, followers of La Négritude believe that from the integration of the civilizations there would be a hope for the realization of a universal humanism.

D. The Social Humanism of Négritude

La Négritude is a social humanism because it is interested in man's relationship with other man and with things (material), as well as in perfecting man's abilities through his own effort.

Man is essentially a producing artist and this is one of the many important attributes that makes him different from animals. Both are products of nature and realize themselves only in and through nature. However, animals do not transform nature and do not aim beyond the satisfaction of subsistence needs. On the other hand, Man realizes himself in nature and through nature. He realizes himself as a human being only by realizing nature, by transforming it to his measure, and by becoming a creator of culture, of civilization. Man, then, has rights – over his activity as a conscious producer, over his expenditure of labor and the objects he produces. The social humanism of La Négritude believes that in a capitalistic system man can undergo alienation and frustration from the fact that he sells to the capitalist his labor power which is the source of all human good. It is not the satisfaction of an inner need for creation, but a means to satisfy needs external to Man.[17]

There is a distinction between Negro-African society and collectivist European society as well. The collectivist Western or European society is an assembly of individuals. It places emphasis on the individual, on his original activity, and his individual needs. In this respect, the subject of potential dispute "*to each according to his labor and to each according to his needs*" is significant.[17a]

Negro-African society tends to put more stress on the group than on the individual, more on solidarity than on the activity and needs of the individual, more on the communion of persons than on their autonomy. Therefore, it is a community, a communal society. This does not mean that it ignores the individual, or that collectivist society ignores solidarity. But the collectivist society bases solidarity on the activities of the individual, whereas the community or communal society bases it on the general activity of the group. The individual in the Western or European societies is the man who distinguishes himself in his basic originality. The member of the community or communal society also claims his autonomy to affirm himself as a being. However, he feels and thinks that he can develop his potential, his originality, only in and by society and in union with all other men.[17b]

Humanism is what we end with and not economics. His labor is an assimilation of labor, a transformation of nature, to satisfy his vital needs, just as is animal activity. But, to the extent that he acts on nature and humanizes it, man acts "on his own nature" and humanizes it at the same time. So, he introduces "consciousness and liberty", as well as artistic feeling into his labor. In so doing he distinguishes himself from the animal. Hence, it is thinking man, from whom all present races descend.[(18)]

Moreover, since men multiply and the planet earth is a closed surface they are compelled to "adjust" lest they be "crushed". To adjust by multiplying their social relations, by sharing their reflections, their instruments, and techniques, and above all by cooperation to invent new thoughts, new techniques, new instruments so as to allow a better adjust. Therefore, it is the scientific answers, the organization of human relations, the reconstruction of the earth – of nature for the promotion of a new human society. By human society is meant not one nation, not one race, not one continent, but all men without exception in a joint effort of organization and reconstruction.[(19)]

So, men grouped together in society under the interacting activity of labor and verbal articulation thanks to the hand extended by the tool and to the brain extended by the senses. This society (a decisive phase of development by consisting of mutual action and complementary activities among human beings) will give birth to civilization. What indeed is civilization but the adoption of nature to man and of man to nature, man's domestication of nature and nature's rapid transformation of man? Transformation not only from his basic to more complex needs; but also, transformation of his ability to think more smartly from a "quantitatively and qualitatively" point of view. This critical beginning would move civilization to a higher level of human advancement and progression.[(20)]

The society of the Negro-African is therefore founded upon a social humanism based on respect for the human being and the society in which he exists. It is founded on something uniquely Negro-African, rejecting communism which in the name of happiness for man reduces him to a slave of society and production; as well as capitalism which in the name of freedom for man allows the most healthy, gifted, and wealthy human beings to roll about in material and moral indulgence (that is excesses).[(21)]

Thus, the essence of Négritude is the practical acceptance of human equality – that is, the equal duty and responsibility to work and contribute to society to the limit of one's capability. Therefore, Négritude is an art of governing men, of a given society, by organizing relations harmoniously.

Footnote:

1. "*The Négritude Movement*", by Gemma Bird. Oxford Research Encyclopedias, in African History. Oxford University Press 2024. Published online: 20 March 2024.
2. David A, Apter, Ideology and Discontent, *p. 189,* (London: The Free Press of Glencoe, 1964).

3ab. A. J. Shelton, p. 121.

4. Paul E. Sigmund Jr., The Ideologies of Developing Countries (New York: Frederick A. Praeger, 1963), p. 248.
5. Leopold S. Senghor (Translated by Mercer Cook), On African Socialism (New York: Frederick A. Praeger, 1964), pp. 158-159.
6. Paul E. Sigmund Jr., p.25.
7. William J. Hanna, p. 533.

8ab. Leopold S. Senghor, "*The Function and Meaning of the First World Festival of Negro Arts*", African Forum, Published by the American Society of the African Culture (Spring 1966), Vol. 1, No, 4, pp. 5-10.

9ab. L. S. Senghor, Liberte: Négritude et Humanism, p. 95.

10. Perspective, pp. 48-49.

11. Frantz Fanon (Translated by Constance Farrington), The Wretched of the Earth (New York: Grave Press, Inc., 1968), pp. 210-213.
12. Ibid, p. 235.
13. David E. Apter, pp. 192-193.
14. L. S. Senghor, On African Socialism, p. 63.

15abc. Ibid, pp. 80-83 and David E. Apter, pp. 191-192, 264.

16. David E. Apter, pp. 192-193.

17ab. L. S. Senghor (Translated by Mercer Cook), On African Socialism, pp. 30-32.

18. David E. Apter, pp. 177-178.
19. L. S. Senghor, Liberte: Negritude et Humanism, pp. 37, 137.
20. Ibid., p.112.
21. "The Dakar Colloquium: Search for a Definition", Africa Report, p. 24.

[illegible]

[illegible] Fanon (Translated by Constance Farrington). The Wretched of the Earth (New York: Grove Press, Inc., 196[illegible]), [illegible]

[illegible]

[illegible]

[illegible]

[illegible]

[illegible]

[illegible]

[illegible]

[illegible]

[illegible]

[illegible]

[illegible]

Chapter VII

The Practical Applicability of La Négritude

The Négritude movement played significant roles on different fronts - as for example in influencing African independence from colonizers by awakening African identity, fostering anti-colonial sentiment, mobilizing intellectuals, influencing politics, gaining international recognition, and leaving an indelible (or enduring) mark on history.

Though it is hard these days to find a Sub-Saharan Negro-African political party embracing La Négritude as a comprehensive, complete, and specific ideological platform and program, **it still remains** relevant in regard to:

- contemporary discussions, especially as it relates to the ongoing issues of race and identity;
- fighting colonial oppression (or neo-colonial as some would now call it) where it still exists in Negro-Africa;
- serving as a historical and intellectual foundation; and,
- inspiring a generation seeking to understand what their aim in life is all about.

There is no doubt that La Négritude left an enduring legacy and remains woven into the fabric of Africanism, and especially Sub-Sahara Negro-Africa.

As the practical applicability of La Négritude is examined, it shall be important to explore how this movement still resonates, even today, in our understanding of Black Africa and African identity.

This chapter shall strive to link the Ideology of Négritude to the socio-historical conditions, which were covered in previous chapters, in order to identify the facts of reality, or the reaction to which this reality exists. Therefore, it will endeavor to answer why people, and leaders in particular, search for an exemplary framework to formulate, think about, establish, and react to problems.

A. Why a Social Humanism as La Négritude?

No other continent in its entirety was so perversely and improperly governed by Europeans, heard its exploitation so often justified on ground of the inborn inferiority of its people, had its modern economy so directly linked to Europe, generally remains in such economic dependence, and in most cases derives its modern language and its modern ideas from abroad than the African Continent. Clearly, the reason why there is the need for an African character, implying that Africa must inevitably be different.

Moreover, many Africans have already discovered that nothing is as difficult as developing economically and industrializing. They also know that their most privileged classes are not capitalists, but salaried government officials, technicians, managers, soldiers, clerks, skilled workers. A social pyramid thus peaked would imply a prospering socialist country, but in Africa it adds up to continuing misery for the majority. Therefore, African leaders have their own set of problems and they must find their own styles and solutions keyed to these problems.[(1)]

Also, certain ambiguities prevail in regard to the nation-states created in Sub-Sahara Africa by the colonizers, that disregarded tribal affiliations which eventually created conflicts because of parochial and universal pulls. Today, in no other continent, does tribalism emerge so painfully as an obstacle to unity, nowhere else is continental unity so obviously a self-made means for overcoming that scarcity which has so far reduced Africa to the sharing of the hazards of sacrificing rather than for progressing.[(2)]

In this period of "decolonization", Negro-Africans are developing their own ideology to meet their several needs which must fill the gap left by the achievement of independence, and set post-independence goals, limits, and guides for action. It must also help define the identity of new nations, most of which have no consistent borders and ethnic communities with little sense of nationhood.[(3)]

Therefore, the new affirmation shall be born out of the crisis of the Negro-African conscience in search of an identity. This crisis would produce the basis for an ideology whose aim shall be to contain the traditional Negro-African roots and experience of its diverse people (be it of any spiritual persuasion as well as ethnic group whether European or otherwise), and employ them for the harmonious growth and development of their society.[(4)]

Here the word **Négritude** is convenient. Devoted to man's need and growth, the word is concerned with man and not simply economics. It stresses the importance of the meaning of love. The stress to establish a priority for the politics of love, or at least to ethical values, is because the majority of today's Negro-African states cannot find enough resources to be able to establish a priority related to material achievement.[5a]

Moreover, Négritude is convenient because it allows Negro-Africans a certain degree of ideological neutrality. In most of Africa the term "capitalism" is unacceptable because, on the one hand, for most Africans, capital is foreign owned and so they associate capitalism with colonialism – or neocolonialism; on the other hand, capitalism in Africa connotes exploitation of men by men. As for "communism", it is also unacceptable, because most Africans see it as another foreign attempt to undercut their independence and another type of materialistic satisfaction.[5b]

Hence, it is possible to say that Negritude is not communist. Négritude is not communist because of communism's materialistic and deterministic basis and implications. Also, it is not communist for a practical reason: the anxiety caused to human dignity and the need for freedom – man's freedoms, and freedoms of the collectivity. Therefore, there is a "*thirst for freedom and hunger for spiritual nourishment*". But, it is not anti-communist, because it can have but one result: increased tension between East and West, and a continuation of the Cold War under another name, with the evident risk of stimulating a third global conflict from which humanity would not recover.[6]

Négritude has the advantage of also being connected with two basic ideas that provided the impulse to the Negro-African independence movements and which still remain post-independence goals: equality and a better future. To this is added the Negro-African aspect of solidarity. It is the solidarity of the kinship group, most evident at the local level. The post-independence task, as most Negro-African leaders see it, is to preserve the sense of community found in the extended family, spread it throughout the whole society, and harness it to the political and economic development plans. In other words, it is, for instance, the concept of the communitary society of Nyerere, or that of the commun-aucratic society of Sekou Toure, or of Senghor's communitarian society.(7)

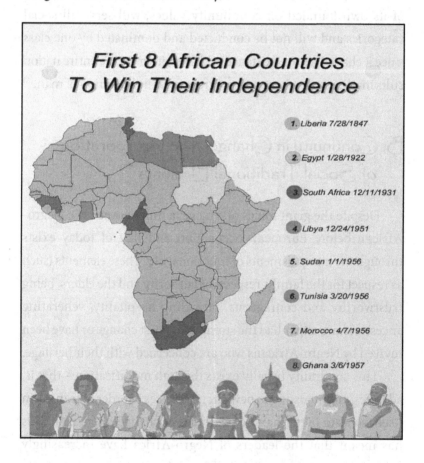

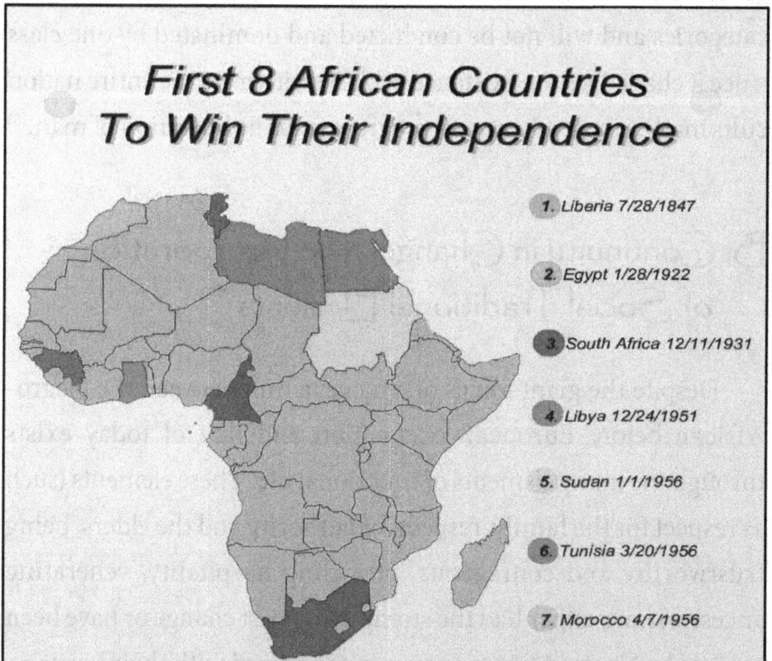

Hence, Negro-African development is characterized by the basic conception of man. Not individualistic man, but "*l'homme personaliste*", who finds his full flowering in the coherence of a living society, of an organic society which relies on the most authentic of traditional Negro-African values for achieving such a goal. That is why the way to development leads also to a community centered not by coercion but by solidarity of free adhesion and free cooperation. As a result, the practical conclusion is that Negro-Africa, by creating a harmonious and total ideology of its own founded on community values, will serve all social categories and will not be conducted and dominated by one class since it challenges the existence of classes; it serves the entire nation culminating in development, progress, and the liberation of man.[(8)]

B. Continuity in Change; The Incorporation of Social Traditional Elements

Despite the giant forces of change, a link between the Negro-African before European occupation and that of today exists through the many elements of traditional life. These elements (such as respect for the family, respect for authority and the elders, being trustworthy and courageous, providing hospitality, venerating ancestry) have either had the strength to resist change or have been revived by Negro-Africans who are concerned with their heritage.

This continuity usually exists through modification – that is, adapting and adjusting to new circumstances in order to transform itself, so as to better handle the forces of change. In general, this has meant that the leaders of Negro-Africa have increasingly sought to incorporate elements from their traditions into more modern concepts of an emerging and developing society.[(9a)]

The reason for such selective policy would be **(a)** that traditional systems are able to help identify what might otherwise be links with the nation and the new leaders, whereas **(b)** some aspects of tradition could bridge the gap between modernity and tradition. Thus, it would add traditional legitimacy to the position of the new Africa, it would lessen the insecurities of rapid change and, by the same token, strengthen the sense of individual and national identity, As one puts it: "*To build the unity of the nation, to give it the psychological strength to be modern, the modernizing elite must in part reassert tradition and reinforce traditional institutions.*[9b]

There are, therefore, two aspects that are necessary for traditional society to efficiently change and for Negro-African leaders to embrace: (a) continuity and (b) adaptation. Not only must certain elements be preserved, but others must be adapted to fit modern social structures and situations. And … Négritude tries to do exactly this.[10]

C. The Problem and Need For Continental Identity

The need for African continental identity (especially Sub-Saharan) is of extreme importance as it re-appropriates or reclaims the racially loaded term of "nègre" to make it a marker of pride in Black identity. In doing so, it needs to challenge the Eurocentric norms and stereotypes that have been an impediment, a barrier, to the growth of the Negro-African and its societies as it emphasizes the uniqueness of the African identity.

Negro-African leaders have been searching for a common denominator that would bring to light its African uniqueness, which would create a concept to formulate an ideology that stresses the identity of the people of the continent while rejecting dominance of the outside world. But agreement on a common concept, by all or at least some, has not yet materialized, has not yet come to fruition.

Négritude developed to replace the outmoded unifying influence of anti-colonialism which had been a powerful force for organizing the Negro-African people during the pre-independence period. With independence there was the need to find new concepts, new doctrines that would continue to unify the Negro-African population. Several approaches were attempted based on concepts such as "nationalism" and "neo-colonialism", but none have been found to be completely adequate and effective. Nevertheless, the form of consciousness that has emerged with a high degree of significance (although, for the moment, with little organizational power and constructive or positive authority) has been that of Négritude, of Africanness, of Blackness.[(11)]

Part of the search for identity consists of discovering, as said before, roots of Negro-African values (as for example: the egalitarian character of society represented by Elders and a Chief or the low degree of stratification, and the extensive network of social obligations that led to considerable cooperation). Not only do these represent a set of roots but, it is thought, that their existence would facilitate the creation and development of modern institutions.[(12)]

Yet, Continental Unity (such as a United States of America, a European Union, or a Russian Federation) has hardly progressed, for although some leaders honestly want it, some use it only as an emotional substitute in internal (that is domestic) politics for the independence which has now been realized, while others are against any form of unity but are afraid to denounce it. In addition, a problem of another magnitude is that once a person, a leader, has gained power and/or wealth, it becomes difficult for that person to share or relinquish it voluntarily. Although there are probably some Negro-African leaders who expect to profit personally from African unity, most look to the possibility of losing power and wealth.(13)

However, even so, of crucial significance is that Négritude attempts and strives to strengthen the Brotherhood and its solidarity within a larger context, a larger unified group, which surpasses ethnic and national differences, which discovers a "common community", and which asserts that *"Africanism reflected in Négritude binds us together to promote the unity and solidarity of the Negro-African"*. In other words, Négritude looks upon all of Mankind as members of an extended family. Under this "Ujamaa" or familyhood, the individual works for the community, and the community cares for the needs of the individual. In contrast to pre-colonial Africa, however, contemporary African States can no longer confine the idea of family to a tribe or a nation-state. Rather, African States, through the Ideology of Négritude, must extend the principles of familyhood and sharing of wealth to the whole African continent(14)

Finally, the need for Continental Unity which Négritude depicts stems from the belief that strength derived from unity will be able to maintain and broaden the freedom acquired since independence.(15)

D. La Négritude and National Reconstruction

One of the main problems that became apparent after independence was that of reconstruction and restoration, because the boundaries of nation-states in Sub-Sahara Africa are artificially demarcated and do not take into account the ethnic and parochial units (in other words, the boundaries that were established by the colonialists to form new states did not take into account original and traditional tribal groups but instead cut across them so that the same tribe was found in two or more countries instead of in one). The ideology of Négritude affirms explicitly, the necessity for Negro-Africa to recognize, determine, and establish a real, vivid unity.

Négritude believes that the fatherland is the heritage handed down by the ancestors: a land, a blood, a language, mores, customs, art, folklore – in a word a native soil, a tribe, an ethnicity, a race. Therefore, the fatherlands would group together in order to transcend the nation-states. It is a "conscious will" to integrate and reconstruct. Objectively, it is a restructuring, along the lines, for instance, of an illustrative model. But to attain this objective, the nation-state must inspire all its members, all individuals with faith in nationhood over and above the fatherlands.[16a]

The "conscious will to integrate", far from rejecting the realities of the fatherland, would as nation-states lean on the individuals within them precisely for their emotional strength, thereby selecting those virtues which by reason of climate, history, or race, share a common denominator or a universal value. Once achieved, the nation forges a harmonious ensemble out of its different parts: a single nation for a single people, animated by one faith and striving toward some goal. In the words of Georg Wilhelm Friedrich Hegel (1770-1831), the theoretician of the nation-state, "*it is not the natural limits of the nation that form its character, but rather its national spirit.*[16b]

As can be inferred, Négritude believes that the nation is

superior to the fatherlands, especially in terms of efficiency. It distills the values of the fatherlands; it sublimates them by transcending them. Hence, the road to nationhood is important because it will forge an action which can make of the various populations a people (that is to say a community) where each individual will identify himself or herself with the collective whole and the collective whole with the individual.(17)

Here then, it can be seen that Négritude is a message to reconstruct and to bring harmony between the individual and the general interest. Therefore, it attempts to integrate all the elements that are still heterogeneous (diverse) in an organic whole.

Hence, as long as integration displays the creation of higher loyalties that supersede parochial loyalties over sub-national communities, tribes, language groups, or regions, it is a universally acclaimed goal of Négritude. Hence, this becomes a universally acclaimed goal of Négritude as long as integration displays the creation of higher loyalties that supersede parochial loyalties over sub-national communities, tribes, language groups, or regions.(18)

To conclude, reconstruction, from an African perspective, is an indispensable antecedent (a forerunner) to the nation, since it is placed as the first reality of the 21st century; it manifests a first tentative to surpass the blind attachment of man to his territory.

E. The Crisis of Economic Development

A major dilemma of Negro-Africa arises from the dependence of African economics on the exports of primary products (inheriting in many cases monocultural economies linked to external – outside of Africa - metropolitan consumers), and from the lack of a developed industrial society. Négritude is committed to industrialization and modernization, and to a reduction of this dependency.[(19a)]

But, the people still remember the harshness and misery that were brought about by the colonialists. Therefore, with the need for industrialization there must be a conviction that this time it will be the people who will benefit - that wealth will not be used for the purpose of acquiring power and prestige by a few, and that ruthless competition among individuals for the purpose of increasing wealth shall be at a minimum (if any). Rather, this time development and its offspring, the increase of wealth for the community's prosperity, shall be used for the satisfaction of needs and for the absolute reduction of poverty.[(19b)]

Another role Négritude plays in economic development is that of the principle of the "state as a father". This depicts the fact that in traditional Negro-African society the Family Chief or the Village Chief was responsible for the way the interests of the society were planned. No individual owned anything; rather it was the society, the commune, the tribe, which owned everything. Individuals worked together in cooperation and in solidarity so as to ripen the fruits of the society; and, everybody was equal.[(20a)]

In short, there was an emphasis on the satisfaction of the simple needs (food, shelter, clothing, education, etc.) and the welfare of the community as a whole with a stress on humanistic values. Therefore, exploitation of men by men hardly existed and the true purpose of wealth was to bring light to the darkness of poverty. It is from this that stems the role of the government in "planning", in providing capital, in guiding the economy, and stressing the "classless society" since social classes are considered to be regarded as self-interested rather than as contributors to the general welfare.[(20b)]

In addition, Négritude seeks to revive other aspects of the traditional Negro-African society, which would be of help to most. For instance, it would reassert the idea of the social obligation to work (in pre-colonial society work was a social obligation. No human being was idle). In so doing parasitism and idleness become social sins, their only effect is to help decrease the material well-being of society and causing economic development to slow down.[(21)]

Thus, as one can see, Négritude is also identified with economic development and shows how and in what way it can affect present day Negro-African society.

F. The Dilemmas of Control and Class Formation

The drive for independence, and eventual economic development following independence, created certain problems of control for the leaders of Negro-Africa resulting in significant challenges to their leadership. While the leaders depended on the populace to achieve their goals they, at the same time, could not understand the important necessity of obtaining the enthusiastic cooperation of the populace – an unfamiliar democratic process.[(22a)]

The new generation of people, and especially those who became leaders, who were brought up during the era of colonialism, learnt from their former European despots (or as some would call them "authoritarian bully dictators") the importance of controlling a dependent people, of leading by subjugating. They did not understand the true meaning of what democracy meant and represented.

Note: Democracy is of Greek origin and consists of two words brought together as one word: "*demos*" meaning people and "*kratos*" meaning rule (in other words, the literal meaning of democracy is "*peoples' rule*" or simply put "rule of the people, by the people, for the people").

For the population as a whole, independence has not been a revolutionary experience, it did not produce change for the better, and it has not provided an improvement in peoples' lives – whether socially, politically, or economically. The colonial governors were gone but many elements of colonialism remained, and attitudes that had been developed in the colonial period continued to be expressed.[22b]

After many decades of being independent nation-states, the end of colonialism did not bring about the expected substantial improvements in the conditions of life for the bulk of the population. For instance, urban problems of unemployment and low standard of living has continued as before, and there is less change in the rural areas (even basic in terms of shelter, food, water quality, health, education, etc.). Moreover, now that European Empires and their controlling power have been dissolved, the natural tendencies begin to assert themselves – the divisive tendencies within the society, the beginning of social classes quarreling and fighting among each other, and the competition between groups, all representing situations that are unsettling and viewed as obstacles to emancipation. Thus, the promises of nationalist leaders have yet to be fulfilled.[23]

In these circumstances, Négritude can be extremely useful for it stresses the identity and values of the Negro-African people while seeking to mobilize the entire population. In this context, it represents a unifying doctrine like the nationalism of the pre-independence period. Moreover, Négritude tries to help create an atmosphere of hard work and self-sacrifice on the part of all elements of the population for the larger collectivity: the nation-state. This is meaningfully put in African traditional terms. There is a general tendency to attempt to promote this experience and to transform the collectivity from the parochial kinship unit to the nation-state. In this respect, Négritude can be a unifying doctrine and may solve certain, if not almost all, the problems of control.(24)

In regard to social classes, they have been recognized with dislike, if not with abhorrence, by many who see them in Negro-Africa as a European import. Society is seen by many as having been with no social strata in its *ideal* pre-foreign contact traditional period. Social classes exploiting one another through the accumulation of capital was not encouraged, was a no-no. As said previously, in traditional Negro-African society everybody was a worker. Even the Elder, who appeared to be enjoying himself without doing much work and for whom everybody else appeared to be working, had, in fact, worked hard all his younger days. The wealth he now appeared to possess was not his personally. He was the guardian of the communal wealth.

The respect paid to him by the younger was earned because he was older and wiser than they and had served his community longer. Consequently, there should be either no classes or the number of social strata should be small, and the differences between the social strata should be minimal. The reason for this line of thought stemmed from the hope of escaping the "class struggle" which accompanied European industrialization and to unite the people under one common goal.[(25)]

Hence, Négritude emphasizes a so-called "classless society" because the idea of a brotherhood or familyhood (in which all men are brethren as members of an ever extending family) leads to harmony and not to conflict within society. This aspect is considered a requirement if rapid development of the nation-state is to be enhanced and disruptive elements are to be considered as constructive criticism (that is gentle). Put in more realistic words, Négritude highlights the fact that the class struggle is not relevant to Africa as it might have been during the period of Europe industrialization.[(26)]

Although there may have been castes or stratifications based on religion, generally speaking, the traditional Negro-African society had no classes founded on individual wealth. This is relevant since the instruments of production belonged to society, the commune, the Tribe. During colonialism, things changed as exploitation created **(a)** a privileged class (the colonialists and their cronies) and **(b)** that of the dispossessed united by their misery. While European workers experienced class subjugation, the mass of African peoples came under racial domination. A major aim of Négritude, therefore, is to ensure that inequalities arising from the "Colonial Pact" are abolished. Because of this potential tendency toward class formation and class warfare, Négritude seeks to restore the communal values of Negro-African society and to revive its humanism.[(27)]

Note: By Colonial Pact it is meant the system of laws and regulations that the colonizing nations imposed on their colonies – meaning that the colonizers were the countries that benefitted from the products and economic activity of their colonial territories.

Thus, Négritude is different from the philosophies or ideologies of the West or East. It holds a view of human nature which rests on fundamental characteristics of the traditional society of Africa: classless, communal, and egalitarian. What is common to these characteristics is the concept that only inside or within a given society can the individual be an accomplished person (that is, successfully achieve); and that the society gives human beings shape, form, and cohesion.[28a]

Unlike the Western Majoritarian conception of democracy, Négritude rejects the "*will of all*" or the "*will of the majority*" and adopts the language of Jean-Jaques Rousseau (1712-1778, a philosopher, writer, and composer who influenced the progress of the Age of Enlightenment throughout Europe) who said: "*the general will, the will of the people*"- meaning the general will (is the will of the sovereign state) and aims at the common good (that is, the good of the community as a whole) as opposed to the "*will of all*" or the "*will of the majority*" which looks out for private interests and is simply the sum of these competing individual interests. Rousseau believed that modern man's enslavement to his own needs was responsible for all sorts of societal ills, from exploitation and domination of others to poor self-esteem and depression.[28b]

Footnote:

1. Manfred Halpern, "African Socialism: Some Unanswered Questions," Africa Report, Vol. 10, No. 10 (November 1965), p. 60.
2. Ibid, p.60.
3. Ruth Schachter Morgenthau, "Declaration of Ideological Independence, "Africa Report, Vol. 8, No. 5 (May 1963), p. 3.
4. Manfred Halpern, p. 62.

5ab. Ibid, pp. 62-63.

6. R. S. Morgenthau, pp. 3-4.
7. I. Wallerstein, pp. 133-134.
8. R. S. Morgenthau, p.4.
9. Richard L. Sklar, "Political Science and National Integration," The Journal of Modern African Studies, Vol. 5, No. 1 (May 1967), pp. 46-47.
10. William J. Hanna, pp. 18-19.
11. W. H. Friedland, and Carl G. Rosberg, African Socialism (Stanford, Cal.: Stanford University Press, 1964), pp. 4-5.
12. Ibid, p. 5.
13. William J. Hanna, pp. 39, 42-43.
14. Ibid, p. 39.
15. Ibid, p.41.

16ab. Perspective, pp. 36-37.

17. R. S. Morgenthau, pp. 3-4, and Perspective, p.38.
18. Richard L. Sklar, pp. 2-3.
19. W. H. Friedland, and Carl G. Rosberg, p. 6.

20ab. W. H. Friedland, "Four Sociological Trends in Africa," Africa Report, Vol. 8, No. 5 (May 1963), pp. 5-6.

21. Ibid, p. 7.

22ab. Donald O'Brien, "*Cooperators and Bureaucrats: Class Formation in African Society*," Africa, Vol. 51, No. 4 (October 1971), p. 175.

23. Donald O'Brien, p. 176.
24. Carl G. Rosberg, and W. H. Friedland, pp. 8-9.

25. R. S. Morgenthau, p.3, and F. Brockway, pp. 29-30.
26. David E. Apter, p. 182.
27. Ibid, p. 178.
28ab. W. H. Friedland, and Carl G. Rosberg, pp. 8-9.

Chapter VIII
Conclusion

La Négritude, as we have seen, starts from certain realities. It tries to unite efforts in a common struggle to eradicate the disparaging image of Negro-Africans, which is the legacy of the slave trade and of the image of being inferior in intellectual capacity and in cultures.

It is a reaction against colonialism which (for many Negro-Africans) brought economic, political, and cultural alienation and estrangement. It is an effort to unite in the struggle against racial discrimination and for self-determination. It tries to detail a logical process of ideas about how the continent should be liberated and reorganized and what the relations of its people should be with other continents – with Europeans, Asians, Americans - and with people of African descent everywhere.

La Négritude represents the Negro-African collective personality. It is not racist, and if it makes itself racist it is because it is an anti-racist racism having as its aim the elimination (if at all possible) of racism.

La Négritude is born out of the crisis of the Negro-African conscience. It is characterized by the fundamental notion of man finding his or her human potential and human development in the integrity and coherence of a living society (i.e., one of bonds formed with others such as family, friends, members of the community, and even strangers). It tries to serve all social classes and the entire nation, culminating in development, progress, and the liberation of mankind.

La Négritude does not appear to be some sort of prototype to erect at any cost and by all means. It is not an end in itself. For Negro-Africans, the full development of their nation-states and the reassertion of the African personality is the sole end, and La Négritude is nothing but a means (a way, a process) to achieve this goal.

La Négritude is not yet a specific guide to action because it does not have a high degree of organizational power as it has neither been directly nor completely embraced by current Sub-Sahara African governments and political parties, though it still remains a powerful testament to the resilience, creativity, and resistance against neo-colonial domination.(1) In addition, it is a viable set of values and dimensions for consciously shaping a historical process; it is a plan for the future as it establishes the bases for a modernized society.

Generally stated, the democratic experience of the West is not necessarily the immediate solution for Africa. It is not an immediate concept to implement in a geographical area, a continent, that has yet to emerge as economically strong with a higher level of education and literacy. Therefore, prior to such a concept being considered, it would be more appropriate for Sub-Sahara Africa to adopt a viable societal transformation, based on the preservation of the Negro-African identity while embracing certain Western values which are compatible to the indigenous ones, and which would allow it to modernize (in other words, mixing the two cultures in a compatible manner). **La Négritude** can help in ensuring that the society is transformed in that way.

Does this mean there can be a middle ground between Western and traditional African systems which are compatible, and when mixed together can provide the required positive energy to modernize? Certainly!

There have been many success stories in Africa and elsewhere (as for example 19th century Japan) who, in their eagerness to develop into viable societies as nation-states, have been able to: **(a)** preserve their cultural and traditional identities while adopting Western values that would motivate and drive them to become industrialized nations and economically strong, and **(b)** allow them, as a consequence, to eventually establish the institutions required to have viable democracies.

Out of the 54 sovereign African countries there are at least 12 who have achieved "varying degrees or levels of development and prosperity": Mauritius, Seychelles, Algeria, Tunisia, Egypt, Morocco, South Africa, Gabon, Botswana, Sierra Leone, Senegal, Malawi. **But,** there are other African countries who are experiencing a more rapid economic growth as for instance Ethiopia, Rwanda, Tanzania, Ivory Coast, Benin, and Ghana - in fact they are among the world's faster growing economies. They have achieved their results by remaining true to their identity and, at the same time, adopt certain Western values (examples of western values: individualism, capitalism, self-reliance, individual freedoms, merit-based society, promoting equal opportunities for individuals, rule of law, electoral governance.).[(2)(3)]

Finding a middle ground between Western-style and traditional African systems involves recognizing the strengths of both approaches and adapting them to local contexts.[(4)]

Here are some considerations:

- **Customization and Hybrid Models:**
    - African nations can customize democratic institutions to suit their unique cultural, historical, and social realities.
    - Some countries have experimented with hybrid models that blend democratic principles with indigenous governance structures. For instance:
        - Botswana: Known for its stable democracy, Botswana combines Western-style elections with traditional tribal councils.
        - Ghana: The chieftaincy system coexists with democratic governance, allowing for community participation.

- **Inclusive Decision-Making:**
    - Traditional African systems often emphasize communal decision-making, consensus building, and respect for elders.
    - These values can complement Western democratic practices, fostering inclusivity and grassroots participation.

- **Decentralization and Local Autonomy:**
    - Empowering local communities through decentralized governance can bridge the gaps or differences.
    - Devolving or transferring authority to regional and local levels allows for tailored solutions and responsiveness to local needs.

- **Cultural Relevance and Identity:**

  - African societies value cultural identity and heritage. Integrating these aspects into governance can enhance legitimacy.
  - Recognizing customary law alongside formal legal systems ensures cultural continuity.

    Customary law is a set of laws based on the traditions, customs, or norms of a local community. In many countries, it is often applied in conjunction with civil, common, and religious legal systems.

- **Economic Development and Social Welfare:**

  - Balancing democratic accountability with economic development is crucial.
  - Policies should address poverty, education, healthcare, and infrastructure, aligning with both Western and African priorities.

- **Education and Civic Awareness:**

  - Promoting civic education helps citizens understand democratic processes and their rights.
  - Combining Western-style education with traditional knowledge can empower informed citizens.

- In summary, the middle ground lies in embracing the best of both worlds: adapting democratic principles while respecting African cultural values. It is an ongoing process that requires dialogue, flexibility, and a commitment to inclusive governance.[5]

What challenges to these African countries still face (and others not mentioned here who are at the very beginning of their modernization curve)?[6]

While the African countries mentioned above have made significant progress, they still face various significant challenges. Here are some common issues:

- **Economic Inequality**: Despite growth, income disparities persist. Many citizens in these countries still struggle with poverty, lack of access to quality education, and limited job opportunities.
- **Corruption**: Corruption remains a challenge across the continent. Some governments struggle to address it effectively, hindering development and public trust.
- **Healthcare**: Access to quality healthcare is uneven. While some countries have made strides, others still grapple with inadequate infrastructure, healthcare worker shortages, and disease outbreaks.
- **Education**: Although progress has been made, education systems face challenges such as overcrowded classrooms, outdated curricula, and insufficient resources that inhibit the ability to significantly increase the level of literacy.
- **Infrastructure**: Roads, electricity, and water supply networks need improvement. The gaps in infrastructure hinder economic growth and social development – especially in rural areas.

- **Political Stability**: Some countries face political instability, ethnic tensions, and conflicts. Maintaining peace and democratic governance remains crucial.
- **Climate Change**: African nations are vulnerable to the impacts of climate change. Droughts, floods, and desertification affect agriculture and livelihoods.
- **Gender Equality**: Gender disparities persist in education, employment, and decision-making. Efforts to empower women and promote gender equality are ongoing. Therefore, equitability or equal opportunities for all is still an issue.
- **Youth Unemployment**: High youth unemployment rates pose challenges. Creating jobs and fostering entrepreneurship are critical.
- **Security**: Some regions deal with terrorism, piracy, and organized crime. Ensuring safety and security is essential for development.

Despite these challenges, the determination of these countries continue to drive progress, and **La Négritude's** legacy persists in contemporary dialogues, inspiring ongoing efforts to dismantle racism, commemorate diversity, and embrace the cause of the marginalized voices. Progress is an ongoing journey, and these countries continue to adapt and innovate in order to take advantage of their opportunities.

In spite of the progress these countries have achieved, they represent only about a third of all the countries in Africa that are on their way to modernization. Generally, though there are definite bright spots, the overall results cannot be called good ... not yet.

This is why the best advice given to Africa still remains the one given by Lord Norman Tebbit, as mentioned in the "Introduction" to this book. As a reminder, he said: "*... we have forgotten the order in which things have to be done. The first priority is the essence – the economy. The second priority is law and order, the freedom from the threat of violence. The third priority is freedom, the ability to order one's own affairs. The fourth priority, the last on the list, is democracy... but too many people think that the list works in reverse. It doesn't.*"

Absolutely correct, only when the economy gets going, and law and order is effectively in place to protect the people from violence and other offenses can freedoms and eventually democracy flourish. Only then rule by the people, of the people, and for the people will prevail.

In conclusion, understanding the plight of Africa requires an all-inclusive holistic, and comprehensive approach that takes into account historical legacies, cultural values, and contemporary realities as an indispensable and a complete framework. The journey toward positive change involves acknowledging both issues "challenges and resilience" combined together. Only then, could the established priorities for a better future be implemented effectively and be able to realize the rewards that are critically needed for the fulfillment of the African dream.

Footnote:

1. Neo-colonialism widely defines how former colonial powers continue to exert control over former colonies mainly through economic exploitation and political means, such as providing assistance accompanied by promises of achieving prosperity (typically with strings attached), rather than through direct colonial rule. It tends to be the most intensive and heightened form of colonialism today. (See Encyclopedia Britannica for a detailed definition of Neo-Colonialism).
2. "*The Wealthiest African Countries in 2023 Ranked by GDP,*" Published by A Rai of Light. February 25, 2023.
3. "*Most Developed Countries in Africa 2024*", World Population Review 2024 Website.
4. "Comparing Western And African Democracy: Challenges And Opportunities – An Analysis", by TransConflict. Eurasia Review News & Analysis. September 3, 2015.
5. *Retrieved from Microsoft Copilot AI-powered assistant.* Microsoft Copilot. (May 14, 2024).
6. "*What Are the Challenges to Economic Growth? And What are the 5 biggest risks facing sub-Saharan Africa this year*", World Economic Forum, Sep 3, 2019.

Bibliography

BOOKS

Amir Tsarfati, with forward by David Jeremiah "*The Last Hour: An Israeli Insider Looks at the End Times*". Published by Chosen Books in 2018, Kindle Edition.

Apter, David E. Ideology and Discontent. London: The Free Press of Glencoe, 1964.

Barnshaw, John (2008). "Race" In Schaefer, Richard T. (ed.). *Encyclopedia of Race, Ethnicity, and Society, Volume 1.* SAGE Publications.

"*Biblical Geography,*" Catholic Encyclopedia: "The ethnographical list found in the Bible's Book of Genesis Chapter 10 is a valuable contribution to the knowledge of the old general geography of the East."

Bill Cooper, "*The Early History of Man Part 1: The Table of Nations*", EN Tech. J., vol. 4, 1990.

Britannica Online, "Language: Characteristics of Language: Historical Attitudes Toward Language," at www.britannica.com/topic/language, By Robert Henry Robins, Published: July 26, 1999 and Updated: December 17, 2021

Brockway, Fenner. African Socialism. Pennsylvania: Dufour Editions, 1963.

Burns, Robert M. (2006). Historiography: Foundations. Taylor & Francis. "The Old Cultural History".

Charles F. Pfeifer. The Wycliffe Bible Commentary, Chicago: Moody Press, 1962.

Charles Freeman, The Greek Achievement: The Foundation of the Western World (New York: Penguin, 1999).

"*Copts And Moslems Under British Control; A Collection Of Facts And A Résumé Of Authoritative Opinions On The Coptic Question*" by Mikhail, Kyriakos, published in 1911 by Smith, Elder & Co., London, England.

David Brion Davis, Inhuman Bondage: The Rise and Fall of Slavery in the New World (Oxford University Press, 2006); Jack Goody, Slavery in Time and Space, in Asian and African Systems of Slavery, ed. James L. Watson (Berkley and Los Angeles: University of California Press, 1980).

Demel, Walter (1 November 2012). Race and Racism in Modern East Asia: Western and Eastern Constructions. *Volume 1 of Brill's Series on Modern East Asia in a Global Historical Perspective.* Publisher BRILL 2012.

Edith Louisa Butcher. *The Story of the Church of Egypt: Being an Outline of the History of the Egyptians Under Their Successive Masters From The Roman Conquest Until Now.* Published in1897 by Smith, Elder, & Co., England.

Fage, John. A History of Africa. Routledge. January 2015

Fanon, Frantz. The Wretched of the Earth. (Translated by Constance Farrington). New York: Grove Press, Inc., 1968.

Fenner Brockway, African Socialism (Pennsylvania: Dufour Editions, 1963).

Founder and Editor: Douglas Harper (November 2001). "*Online Etymological Dictionary*".

Fred P. Von der Mehden, Politics of the Developing Nations (Englewood Cliffs, N.J.: Prentice Hall, Inc., 1964).

Friedland, W. H., and Rosberg, Carl G. (Editors). African Socialism. Stanford, Cal.: Stanford University Press, 1964.

Hanna, William John. Independent Black Africa: The Politics of Freedom. Chicago: Rand McNally and Company, 1964.

Heller, Eva (2009). Psychologie de la couleur – Effets et symboliques. Pyramyd (French translation)

Herodotus Histories III.114 English translation by A. D. Godley. Cambridge. Harvard University Press. 1920

"*Histoire de l'Eglise d'Alexandrie*", by R.P. Georges Macaire, Le Caire, 1894.

"*Histoire de l'Egypte Sous Mohammed Aly*", by Felix Mengin, Paris, 1923.

"*Histoire de Mehmet Ali, Vice-Roi d'Egypte*", by Paul Mouriez, Paris, 1858.

Iddrisu, Abdulai (6 January 2023). "*A Study in Evil: The Slave Trade in Africa*"

Ira Berlin, a leading historian of the history of slavery in North America and the Atlantic World. Many Thousands Gone: The First Two Centuries of Slavery in North America. Published by Harvard University Press, 1998.

J. H. Kautsky, Political Change in Underdeveloped Countries: Nationalism and Communism (New York: John Wiley and Sons Inc.,1967).

July, Robert W. The Origins of Modern African Thought. New York: Frederick A. Praeger, 1967.

Kalisch, Marcus M., *A Historical and Critical Commentary of the Old Testament,* London, UK, Longmans, Brown, Green, 1858.

Kautzsch, Prof., quoted by James Orr, "*The Early Narratives of Genesis,*" in The Fundamentals, vol.1, Biola Press, 1917.

Kautsky, J. H. Political Change in Underdeveloped Countries: Nationalism and Communism. New York: John Wiley and Sons Inc., 1967.

Kennedy, Rebecca F. (2013). "Introduction". Race and Ethnicity in the Classical world: An Anthology of Primary Sources in Translation. Hackett Publishing Company.

Frantz Fanon (Translated by Constance Farrington), The Wretched of the Earth (New York: Grave Press, Inc., 1968).

"*Les Familles Coptes Du Caire: Famille Ghali*", by H.L. Rabino and published by Imprimerie D. Spada, 1937

"*Le Statut Personnel des Non Musulmans*", Le Caire, 1937; "*La Protection Religieuse En Egypte*", Le Caire, 1937. Les deux livres sont écrits par Ragheb Bey Ghali

Lewis, Martin W.; Wigen, Kären (1997). The myth of continents: a critique of metageography. *Berkeley and Los Angeles: University of California Press.* Lewis & Wigen 1997.

Liddell, Henry George; Scott, Robert. "Aithiops". A Greek-English Lexicon. Perseus. 2 December 2017.

Mann, Stuart E. (1984). An Indo-European Comparative Dictionary. Hamburg: Helmut Buske Verlag.

Mediterranean, the Barbary Coast and Italy (1500-1800)", Palgrave Macmillan.

Mehden, Fred R. Von der. Politics of the Developing Nations. Englewood Cliffs, N. J.: Prentice Hall, Inc., 1964.

Pastoureau, Michael (2008). *Black: The History of a Color*. Princeton University Press.

Pastoureau, Michel (2008). *Noir – Histoire d'une couleur*, Publisher LE SEUIL, 2017.

Paul E. Sigmund Jr., The Ideologies of Developing Countries (New York: Frederick A. Praeger, 1963).

"*Merveilles Biographique et Historiques*" du cheikh Abd el-Rahman al-Djabarti. Traduction Française, Le Caire, T. VII, 1892, T. VIII, 1895, T. IX, 1896.

Race In Schaefer, Richard T. (ed.). "*Encyclopedia of Race, Ethnicity, and Society*", *Volume 1.* SAGE Publications.

Richard Alburtus Morrisey. Bible History of the Negro. Originally Published 1915, Publisher: Independently published (May 7, 2020), Kindle Edition.

Richard Sandbrook, The Politics of Africa's Economic Stagnation, Cambridge University Press, 1985.

Robert C. Davis (2003). Christian Slaves, Muslim Masters: White Slavery in the Mediterranean, the Barbary Coast, and Italy, 1500–1800. Published by Palgrave Macmillan

Robert Hetzron, "Afroasiatic Languages" in Bernard Comrie, The World's Major Languages, 2009.

Robert A. July, The Origin of Modern African Thought (New York: Frederick A. Praeger, 1967).

Rogers, Jeffrey S. (2000), p.1271. *"Table of Nations". In Freedman, David Noel; Myers, Allen C. (eds.). Eerdmans Dictionary of the Bible. Amsterdam University Press.*

Rufus Lewis Perry. Early Settlements of the Cushites, The Cushite, or The Descendants of Ham. Published in 1893.

Rufus Lewis Perry. "Color of the Egyptians", The Cushite Or The Descendants Of Ham, published in 1893.

Russell Thornton, American Indian Holocaust and Survival: A Population History Since 1492 (University of Oklahoma Press, 1987).

Sayre, April Pulley *(1999),* Africa*, Twenty-First Century Books.*

Senghor, Leopold Sedar. Liberte: Négritude et Humanisme. Paris: Editions de Seuil, 1964. Frantz Fanon (Translated by Constance Farrington), The Wretched of the Earth (New York: Grave Press, Inc., 1968).

Senghor, Leopold Sedar. On African Socialism. (Translated by Mercer Cook). New York: Frederick A. Praeger, 1964.

Sidney & Shirley Robbins. Africa: A Continent in Agony - We Accuse, (Published 2012 as an eBook, Capsal Publishers).

Sigmund, Paul E. The Ideologies of Developing Countries. New York: Frederick A. Praeger, 1961.

St. Clair, Kassia (2016). The Secret Lives of Colour. London: John Murray. The Cambridge Encyclopedia of Language, Cambridge University Press; 3rd edition (July 26, 2010), Principal Author: David Crystal, honorary professor of linguistics at the University of Wales, OBE, FBA, FLSW, FCIL is a British linguist, academic, and author.

The Poverty of Leadership in Africa, The Fate of Africa: From the Hopes of Freedom to the Heart of Despair: A History of Fifty Years of Independence, Martin Meredith.Vol.26, No.2 (Summer-Fall 2006). Published By: The Johns Hopkins University Press

Wallerstein, I. The Politics of Independence. New York: Alfred A. Knopff, Inc., 1961.

W. H. Friedland, and Carl G. Rosberg, African Socialism (Stanford, Cal.: Stanford University Press, 1964).

Wilson, Nigel (2013). Encyclopedia of Ancient Greece. Routledge. 2016.

William J. Hanna, Independent Black Africa: The Politics of Freedom (Chicago: Rand McNally and Company, 1964).

Zimmermann, K. (2008). "Lebou et Libou ». Encyclopédie berbère. 28-29 | Kirtēsii – Lutte. Aix-en-Provence: Edi Sud.

Zuffi, Stefano. Color in Art, Publisher: Abrams (June 1, 2012)

PERIODICALS, ARTICLES AND VIDEOS

1799 James Rennell map with the Aethiopian Sea in the Gulf of Guinea area.

"*2020 Alphabetical List of All African Countries*" By Angela Thompsell (Professor of British and African History), published by Thought Co. – an Internet company.

Abdoulie Janneh (April 2012). "Item 4 of the provisional agenda – General debate on national experience in population matters: adolescents and youth (Pdf). United Nations Economic Commission For Africa. Retrieved 15 December 2015.

"*Africa*", Encyclopedia Britannica. Africa | History, People, Countries, Map, & Facts | Britannica https://www.britannica.com/place/Africa by Alfred Kröner (Contributor)

"*Africa Can Feed Itself in a Generation, Experts Say*", Science Daily, December 3, 2010.

"*Afro-Asiatic languages*". Encyclopedia Britannica, Published: 25 May 2020

"All Africa: Developed Countries' Leverage on the Continent". AllAfrica.com. February 7, 2008.

"*A Statement on Race and Racism*" from the American Association of Biological

Anthropologists (formerly AAPA), 27 March 2019.

Antonia Cirjak. How Do Race And Ethnicity Affect Identity?, in Society World Atlas, June 2, 2020.

"*Are black people cursed*?" by Got Questions Ministries, Colorado Springs, Colorado. Barnshaw, John (2008).

Austin J. Shelton, "*The Black Mystique: Reactionary Extremes in Negritude*", African Affairs, Vol. 69 (April 1964).

"*Barbary: Historical Region, Africa*", *by Michael Brett*. The Editors of Encyclopedia

Britannica. December 14, 2021.

Brantlinger, Patrick (1985). "*Victorians and Africans*: The Genealogy of the Myth of the Dark Continent". Critical Inquiry.

C.C. Wrigley, "*Historicism in Africa: Slavery and State Formation*," African Affairs, Vol. 70 (April 1971).

"China tightens grip on Africa with $4.4bn lifeline for Guinea junta". The Times. October 13, 2009.

"*Comparing Western And African Democracy: Challenges And Opportunities – An Analysis*", by TransConflict. Eurasia Review News & Analysis. September 3, 2015.

"*Dakar Colloquium: Search for Definition*," Africa Report, Vol. 8, No. 5 (May 1963).

"*Demography, Geography, and the Sources of Roman Slaves*", by W.V. Harris, published in the *Journal of Roman Studies*, 1999.

Donald O'Brien, "*Cooperators and Bureaucrats: Class Formation in African Society,*" Africa, Vol. 51, No. 4 (October 1971).

Evans, William M (February 1980), "*From the Land of Canaan to the Land of Guinea: The Strange Odyssey of the 'Sons of Ham'*", American Historical Review.

Extrait d'une letter du Consul de France Drovetti, au Ministere des Affaires Etrangeres a Paris, date d'Alexandrie, le 22 Mai 1822.

"*How Did Africa Get Its Name*?", African History Videos, Video No. One and Two, Website: www.patreon.com/HomeTeamHistory, 2018 production.

Human Development Report 2023-24. "*Breaking the gridlock: Reimagining cooperation in a polarized world.*" United Nations Development Program, 13 March 2024.

Indult (a privilege granted by the Pope) *du 1er Mai 1807*: Ex-Audientia Smi Nri Pii Divina Providentia PP: VII:habita per me infrum Sacrae Congnis De Propaganda Fide Praefectum Die Prima Maji 1807.

James Clackson (Edited). *Introduction To A Companion to the Latin Language,* Publisher Name: Wiley-Blackwell; 1st edition (2011).

"L'Afrique en Devenir: Essai sur l'Avenir de l'Afrique Noir," Perspective, No. 13 (Juin 1966).

Lettre du Pape Pie VII a Moallem Ghali et Philotheos Yakoub (cousin-germain de Moallem Ghali), 15 Juillet 1807. Extract from the Archives of the Propaganda at Rome (Udienze di N.S. Vol. 45. Fol.365 v.).

"*The Dakar Colloquium: Search for a Definition*," Africa Report, Vol. 8, No, 5 (May 1963).

"*Five Ways The World Will Look Dramatically Different in 2100*", The Washington Post August 17, 2015.

Friedland, W. H. "*Four Sociological Trends in Africa*," Africa Report, Vol. 8, No. 5 (May 1963).

Gates Jr., Henry Louis, "*Opinion: How to End the Slavery Blame Game*". New York Times, April 22, 2010.

George Babington Michell, "*The Berbers*", Journal of the Royal African Society, Vol. 2, No. 6 (January 1903).

Ginio, Eyal. "*Piracy and Redemption in the Aegean Sea During the First Half of the Eighteenth Century*". Published in Turcica Journal, Volume 33 (2001).

Halpern, Manfred. "African Socialism: Some Unanswered Questions," Africa Report, Vol10, No. 10 (November 1965).

"*Historical Foundations of Race*" by David R. Roediger, National Museum of African American History and Culture, Website: https://nmaahc.si.edu/learn/talking-about-race/topics/historical-foundations-race

"*History of Sub-Saharan Africa*". (2022). *Essential Humanities.* Retrieved from http://www.essential-humanities.net/world-history/sub-saharan-africa/

"*Historical Survey: Slave Owning Societies*". Encyclopedia Britannica, 2007.

How Scientific Taxonomy Constructed the Myth of Race" by Kenyon-Flatt, Britanny (March 19, 2021).

"*Human Races Are Not Like Dog Breeds: Refuting A Racist Analogy*" by Norton, Heather; Quillen, Ellen; Bigham, Abigail; Pearson, Laurel; Dunsworth, Holly (July 9, 2019).

J. H. A. Watson, "*French Speaking Africa Since Independence*", <u>African Affairs</u>, Vol. 62 (July 1963).

József Herman, *Vulgar Latin*, translated by Roger Wright (Pennsylvania State University Press, 2000, originally published 1975 in French).

"*Indian Ocean and Middle Eastern Slave Trades*", by George M. La Rue, December 2020, Oxford Bibliographies.

"*L'Afrique en Devenir: Essai sur L'Avenir de L'Afrique Noir,*" Perspective, XIII (June 1966).

"*Making the Distant Past Relevant to the Present Day: Were the Ancient Egyptians Black?*" Website: https://talesoftimesforgotten.com/2020/04/23/ 188 were-the-ancient-egyptians-black/, By Spencer McDaniel, April 23, 2020.

Manfred Halpern, "*African Socialism: Some Unanswered Questions,*" Africa Report, Vol. 10, No. 10 (November 1965).

Merriam-Webster Dictionary.com/dictionary/civilization/ and "*History of Sub-Saharan Africa*". (2022). *Essential Humanities.*

Miran, Jonathan (2022-04-20), "*Red Sea Slave Trade*". Oxford Research Encyclopedia of African History, November 2023.

Morgenthau, Ruth Schochter. "Declaration of Ideological Independence," Africa Report, Vol. 8, No. 5 (May 1963).

"*Nearly Half of the World Lives on Less Than $5.50 A Day.*" The World Bank, Washington D.C., USA. Press Release No. 2019/044/DEC-GPV. October 17, 2018. The World Bank, Washington D.C., USA

O'Brien, Donald. "Cooperators and Bureaucrats: Class Formation in African Society," Africa, Vol. 51, No. 4 (October 1971).

"*Phoenicia Defined*" by Joshua J. Mark, published March, 19, 2018, in World History Encyclopedia, Website: https://www.worldhistory.org/phoenicia/

"*Origin Of The Word Slave*", The American Heritage® Dictionary of the English Language, Fourth Edition, Posted By: Siebra Muhammad, October 31st, 2011

"*Population of Africa (2019)*" by Worldometers – a provider of global statistics.

Reynolds, Susan (October 1983). "*Medieval Origines Gentiuman the Community of the Realm*". *History. Chichester, West Sussex: Wiley-Blackwell.*

Robert I. Rotberg, "*African Nationalism*", The Journal of Modern African Studies, Vol. 4 (May 1966).

Rotberg, Robert I. "African Nationalism," Journal of Modern African Studies, Vol. 4 (May 1966).

Ruth Schachter Morgenthau, "*Declaration of Ideological Independence*", Africa Report, Vol. 8, No. 5 (May 1963).

"*Saqaliba - Slavs in the Arab World*", *Part 3* ("Slavs in Muslim Spain", part (1)", article by Niklot and Marek Kalisiński, Slavik Chronicles, July 2, 2017.

Sene, Alione. "*Negritude et Revolution Africaine,*" Service de Presse et d'Information de l'Ambassade du Senegal au Caire (une conference donnee par l'Ambassadeur du Senegal au Caire au Centre d'Etudes Dar Es Salaam, le 24 Janvier, 1972).

Senghor, Leopold Sedar. "The Function and Meaning of the First World Festival of Negro Arts," African Forum, Vol. 1, No. 4 (Spring 1966).

Shelton, Austin J. "The Black Mystique: Reactionary Extremes in Negritude," African Affairs, Vol. 69 (April 1964).

Sklar, Richard L. "*Political Science and National Integration*," The Journal of Modern African Studies, Vol. 5, No. 1 (May 1967).

"*Slavs of Muslim Spain*", by Michal Warczakowsk, The Apricity: A European Cultural Community, Website: www.theapricity.com, 31.01.2004.

"Scramble for Africa", Encyclopædia Britannica, Inc./Kenny Chmielewski 2024.

Thatcher, Oliver. "*Vasco da Gama: Round Africa to India, 1497-1498.*" Modern History Sourcebook. Milwaukee: University Research Extension Co. February 2018.

The Atlantic Slave Trade, Written by Thomas Lewis. Editor Gloria Lotha The Editors of Encyclopedia Britanica, Inc. Jun 28, 2016.

"*The Berlin Conference of 1884-85*", New World Encyclopedia, dated 29th August 2008.

"*The developing world is poorer than we thought, but no less successful in the fight against poverty*". Published August 26, 2008, by World Bank. Website: www.econ.worldbank.org/external/default/main

"*The Discovery of the Americas and the Transatlantic Slave Trade*". Written and Published by Ira Berlin, a leading historian of the history of slavery in North America and the Atlantic World (9 April 2012).

The Encyclopædia Britannica: A Dictionary of Arts, Sciences, and General Literature, C. Scribner's Sons. 1878.

"*The Négritude Movement*", by Gemma Bird. Oxford Research Encyclopedias, in African History. Oxford University Press 2024. Published online: 20 March 2024.

"*The Origins of Slavery*". Written and Published by Ira Berlin, a leading historian of the history of slavery in North America and the Atlantic World.

"*The Rise and Fall of King Sugar*", National Archives of Trinidad and Tobago. January 2023.

"*The Table of Nations (Genealogy of Mankind) and the Origin of Nations (History of Man)*" by Tim Osterholm, Website: http://www.crystalsoftwaredesign.com/Genealogy/Nations.html

"*The Meaning of Ethnicity: What It Is and How To Use It*", by Kevin Miller, The Word Encounter, June 30, 2022.

"The *Most Developed Countries in Africa 2024*", World Population Review 2024 Website.

"The Way I See It - "The Missing 100+ Million" by Jack Crawford, The Laguna Mobilization 2/21 Writers' Group (USA African Writers), June 6, 2006.

"*The Wealthiest African Countries in 2023 Ranked by GDP,*" Published by A Rai of Light. February 25, 2023.

"*The History of the Trans-Atlantic Slave Trade*", National Museums Liverpool July 2002.

"*United Nations Development Program*", Website: http://hdr.undp.org/

Watson, J. H. A. "French Speaking Africa Since Independence," African Affairs, Vol. 62 (July 1963).

"*Western Colonialism*" by Harry Magdoff, Britannica, 2021 Edition.

W. H. Friedland, "*Four Sociological Trends in Africa,*" Africa Report, Vol. 8, No. 5 (May 1963).

"*What Was The Original Name Of Africa*?", World Atlas, website: www.worldatlas.com dated June 16, 2020.

"What Are the Challenges to Economic Growth? And What are the 5 biggest risks facing sub-Saharan Africa this year", World Economic Forum, Sep 3, 2019.

"*Who Were the Phoenicians?*" by Megan Sauter, Biblical Archaeology Society, October 3, 2021, Website: https://www.biblicalarchaeology.org

Williams, Frank (2008-11-27). The Panarion of Epiphanius of Salamis: Book I: (Sections 1-46) BRILL, Second Edition 2008, Revised and Expanded.

"*Where did the Word Slave Come From?*", Academic General Knowledge, 2023, Website: https://lisbdnet.com/where-did-the-word-slave-come-from/

"*Why did Noah curse Canaan instead of Ham?*" by Got Questions Ministries, Colorado Springs, Colorado.

William J. Tinkle, Genetics Favors Creation, "*Creation Research Society Quarterly*", December 1977.

Wrigley, Christopher. "*Historicism in Africa: Slavery and State Formation,*" African Affairs, Vol. 70, No. 279 (April 1971).

"World Bank Updates Poverty Estimates for the Developing World." World Bank. 26 August 2008.

Yudell, M.; Roberts, D.; DeSalle, R.; Tishkoff, S. "*Taking Race Out of Human Genetics: Engaging a Century-Long Debate About the Role of Race in Science*", (5 February 2016). Science: Vol. 351, No. 6273.

Printed in the United States
by Baker & Taylor Publisher Services